IMAGINATION IN PLACE

Other Books of Essays by Wendell Berry

# Imagination in Place

*Essays*

WENDELL BERRY

COUNTERPOINT · BERKELEY

Copyright © 2010 by Wendell Berry.
All rights reserved under International and Pan-American
Copyright Conventions.

Library of Congress Cataloging-in-Publication Data

Berry, Wendell, 1934–
  Imagination in place : essays / by Wendell Berry.
     p. cm.
  ISBN: 978-1-58243-706-4
  I. Title.

  PS3552.E75163 2010
  814'54—dc22

                                2009038104

Book design by Gopa & Ted2, Inc.
Printed in the United States of America

COUNTERPOINT
1919 Fifth Street
Berkeley, CA 94710

www.counterpointpress.com

Distributed by Publishers Group West

10 9 8 7 6 5 4 3 2 1

# Contents

# Imagination in Place

# Imagination in Place

~

## (2004)

By an interworking of chance and choice, I have happened to live nearly all my life in a place I don't remember not knowing. Most of my forebears for the last two hundred years could have said the same thing. I was born to people who knew this place intimately, and I grew up knowing it intimately. For a long time the intimacy was not very conscious, but I certainly did not grow up here thinking of the place as "subject matter," and I have never thought of it in that way. I have not lived here, or worked with my neighbors and my family, or listened to the storytellers and the rememberers, in order to be a writer. The place is precedent to my work, especially my fiction, and is, as I shall try to show, inevitably different from it.

By the same interworking of chance and choice, though somewhat expectably, I have lived here as a farmer. Except for one great-grandfather, all of my family that I know about have been farming people, and I grew up under instruction, principally from my father but also from others, to learn farming, to know the difference between good farming and bad, to regard the land as of ultimate value, and to admire and respect those who farmed well. I never heard a farmer spoken of as "just a farmer" or a farm woman as "just a housewife." To my father and his father especially, the knowledge of land and of farming was paramount. They thought the difference between a good farmer and a bad one was just as critical as the difference between a good politician and a bad one.

In 1964, after several years of wandering about, my wife Tanya and I returned to Kentucky with our two children and bought the property known as Lanes Landing, on the Kentucky River, about a mile from the house where my mother was born and raised and about five miles from my father's home place. The next summer we fixed up the house and moved in. We have been here ever since. Or Tanya and I have; our children are farming nearby.

Before we moved here, I had known this place for thirty-one years, and we have now lived here for thirty-nine. We raised our children here. We have taken from this place most of our food, much of our fuel, and always, despite the difficulties and frustrations of a farming life, a sustaining pleasure. Also, nearly everything I have written has been written here. When I am asked how all this fits together, I have to say, "Awkwardly." Even so, this has been the place of my work and of my life.

This essay is most immediately obstructed by the difficulty of separating my work from my life, and the place from either. The place included in some of my work is also the place that has included me as a farmer and as a writer.

In the course of my life and of my work as a farmer, I have come to know familiarly two small country towns and about a dozen farms. That is, I have come to know them well enough at one time or another that I can shut my eyes and see them as they were, just as I can see them now as they are. The most intimate "world" of my life is thus a small one. The most intimate "world" of my fiction is even smaller: a town of about a hundred people, "Port William," and a few farms in its neighborhood. Between these two worlds, the experienced and the imagined, there is certainly a relationship. But it is a relationship obscure enough as it is, and easy to obscure further by oversimplification. Another difficulty of this essay is the temptation to oversimplify.

As a lot of writers must know, it is easy for one's family or neighbors to identify fictional characters with actual people. A lot of writers must know too that these identifications are sometimes astonishingly wrong, and are always at least a little wrong. The inevitability of this sort of error is explainable, and it is significant.

Some of my own fiction has seemed to me to be almost entirely imagined. Some of it has drawn maybe as close as possible to actual experience. The writing has sometimes grown out of a long effort to come to terms with an actual experience. But one must not be misled by the claims of "realism." There is, true enough, a kind of writing that has an obligation to tell the truth about actual experience, and therefore it is obliged to accept the limits of what is actually or provably known. But works of imagination come of an impulse to transcend the limits of experience or provable knowledge in order to make a thing that is whole. No human work can become whole by including everything, but it can become whole in another way: by accepting its formal limits and then answering within those limits all the questions it raises. Any reasonably literate reader can understand Homer without the benefit of archaeology, or Shakespeare without resort to his literary sources.

It seems to me that my effort to come to terms in writing with an actual experience has been, every time, an effort to imagine the experience, to see it clear and whole in the mind's eye. One might suppose, reasonably enough, that this could be accomplished by describing accurately what one actually knows from records of some sort or from memory. But this, I believe, is wrong. What one actually or provably knows about an actual experience is never complete; it cannot, within the limits of memory or factual records, be made whole. Imagination "completes the picture" by transcending the actual memories and provable facts. For this reason, I have often begun with an actual experience and in the end produced what I have had to call a fiction. In the effort to tell a whole story, to see it whole and clear, I have had to imagine more than I have known. "There's no use in telling a pretty good story when you can tell a really good one," my mother's father told me once. In saying so, he acknowledged both a human limit and a human power, as well as his considerable amusement at both.

I believe I can say properly that my fiction originates in part in actual experience of an actual place: its topography, weather, plants, and animals; its language, voices, and stories. The fiction I have written here, I suppose, must somehow belong here and must be different from any fiction I might have written in any other place. I am pleased to suppose so, but the issue of influence is complex and obscure, and the influence of this place alone cannot account for the fiction and the other work I have written here.

Both my writing and my involvement with this place have been in every way affected by my reading. My work would not exist as it is if the influence of this place were somehow subtracted from it. Just as certainly it would not exist as it is, if at all, without my literary mentors, exemplars, teachers, and guides. Lists are dangerous, but as a placed writer I have depended on the examples of Andrew Marvell at Appleton House, Jane Austen in Hampshire, Thomas Hardy in Dorset, Mark Twain in Hannibal, Thoreau in Concord, Sarah Orne Jewett on the Maine coast, Yeats in the west of Ireland, Frost in New England, William Carlos Williams in Rutherford, William Faulkner and Eudora Welty in Mississippi, Wallace Stegner in the American West, and in Kentucky, James Still, Harlan Hubbard, and Harry Caudill—to name only some of the dead and no contemporaries. I have kept fairly constantly in my mind the Bible, Homer, Dante, Shakespeare, Herbert, Milton, and Blake. I have taken much consolation and encouragement from Paul Cézanne's devotion to his home landscapes in Provence and from Samuel Palmer's work at Shoreham. I have remembered often the man of Psalm 128 who shall eat the labor of his hands, and Virgil's (and Ronsard's) old Cilician of *Georgics* IV. Over the last twenty years or so, I have contracted a large debt to certain writers about religious and cultural tradition, principally Ananda Coomaraswamy, Titus Burckhardt, Kathleen Raine, and Philip Sherrard—again, to name only the dead. Now that I have listed these names, I am more aware than before how incomplete any such list necessarily must be, and how necessarily confusing must be the issue of influence.

I will allow the list to stand, not as an adequate explanation, but as a hint at the difficulty of locating the origins of a work of fiction by me (or, I assume, by anybody else). And I must add further to the difficulty by saying that I don't believe I am conscious of all the sources of my work. I dislike learned talk about "the unconscious," which always seems to imply that the very intelligent are able somehow to know what they don't know, but I mean only to acknowledge that much of what I have written has taken me by surprise. What I know does not yield a full or adequate accounting for what I have imagined. It seems to have been "given." My experience has taught me to believe in inspiration, about which I think nobody can speak with much authority.

My fiction, anyhow, has come into being within the contexts of local geography and local culture, of the personal culture of reading, listening, and looking, and also within the contexts of what is not known and of the originating power we call inspiration. But there is another context, that of agriculture, which I will need to deal with at more length.

I was brought up, as I have said, by agrarians and was conscientiously instructed in a set of assumptions and values that could be described only as agrarian. But I never saw that word in print or heard it pronounced until I was a sophomore at the University of Kentucky. At that time I was in a composition class whose instructor, Robert D. Jacobs, asked us to write an argument. I wrote, as I recall, a dialogue between two farmers on the condemnation of land for the construction of a highway or an airport. The gist of my argument was that the land was worth more than anything for which it might be destroyed. Dr. Jacobs didn't think much of my argument, but he did me a valuable service by identifying it as "agrarian" and referring me to a group of writers, the Southern Agrarians, who had written a book called *I'll Take My Stand*. I bought the book and read at least part of it about three years later, in 1956. It is a valuable book, in some ways a wonder, and I have returned to it many times since. My debt to it has increased.

I must have become a good deal interested in the Southern Agrarians during my last years at the university, for with my friend and fellow student Mac Coffman (Edward M. Coffman, the historian) I drove up to Kenyon College to talk with John Crowe Ransom on that subject. But it is hard now for me to tell how much I may have been influenced by the Southern Agrarians and their book at that time. (Ransom by then was disaffected from *I'll Take My Stand*, though his elegant introduction, "A Statement of Principles," is still the best summary of agrarian principles versus the principles of industrialism). And I think I encountered not much at the University of Kentucky that would have confirmed my native agrarianism. It seems to me now that my agrarian upbringing and my deepest loyalties were obscured by my formal education. Only after I returned to Kentucky in 1964 did I begin to reclaim what I had been taught at home as a growing boy. Once I was home again, the purpose and point of that teaching became clear to me as it had not before, and I became purposefully and eagerly an agrarian. Moreover, because I had settled here as a farmer, I knew that I was not a literary agrarian merely but also a practical one.

In 1970 I published in *The Southern Review* a small essay, "The Regional Motive," that I suppose was descended from, or at least a cousin to, the essays of *I'll Take My Stand*. But in my essay I said that "the withdrawal of the most gifted of [the Southern Agrarians] into . . . Northern colleges and universities invalidated their thinking, and reduced their effort to the level of an academic exercise." Whatever the amount of truth in that statement, and there is some, it is also a piece of smartassery.

I received in response a letter from Allen Tate. As I knew, Tate could be a combative man, and so I was moved, as I still am, by the kindness of his letter. He simply pointed out to me that I did not know the pressing reasons why he and his friends had moved to the North. And so when I reprinted my essay I added a footnote apologizing for my callowness and ignorance, but saying, even so —and, as I remember, with Tate's approval—that I might appropriately "warn that their departure should not be taken either as disproof of the validity of their [agrarian] principles, or as justification of absentee regionalism (agrarianism without agriculture)."

The parentheses around that concluding phrase suggest to me now that I was making a point I had not quite got. The phrase, which appears to have been only an afterthought thirty-two years ago, indicates what to me now seems the major fault of *I'll Take My Stand*: The agrarianism of most of the essays, like the regionalism of most of them, is abstract, too purely mental. The book is not impractical—none of its principles, I believe, is in conflict with practicality—but it is too often remote from the issues of practice. The legitimate aim (because it is the professed aim) of agrarianism is not some version of culture but good farming, though a culture complete enough may be implied in that aim. By 1970 I had begun to see the flaws and dangers of absentee regionalism, and especially of Southern absentee regionalism. Identifying with "The South," as if it were somehow all one and the same place, would not help you to write any more than it would help you to farm. As a regional book, *I'll Take My Stand* mostly ignores the difficulty and the discipline of locality. As an agrarian book, it mostly ignores also the difficulty and the discipline of farming, but this problem is more complicated, and dealing with it took me longer.

Of the twelve essayists, only Andrew Lytle and John Donald Wade appear to speak directly from actual knowledge of actual farming in an actual place. And a passage of Andrew Lytle's essay, "The Hind Tit," points the direction I now must take with this essay of mine. He has begun to write about "a type" of farmer who has two hundred acres of land, but he does so with a necessary precaution:

> This example is taken, of course, with the knowledge that the problem on any two hundred acres is never the same: the richness of the soil, its qualities, the neighborhood, the distance from market, the climate, water, and a thousand such things make the life on every farm distinctly individual.

Thus he sets forth the fundamental challenge, not only to all forms of industrial land use, but to all other approaches to land use, including agrarianism, that are abstract.

The most insistent and formidable concern of agriculture, wherever it is taken seriously, is the distinct individuality of every farm, every field on every farm, every farm family, and every creature on every farm. Farming becomes a high art when farmers know and respect in their work the distinct individuality of their place and the neighborhood of creatures that lives there. This has nothing to do with the set of personal excuses we call "individualism" but is akin to the holy charity of the Gospels and the political courtesy of the Declaration of Independence and the Bill of Rights. Such practical respect is the true discipline of farming, and the farmer must maintain it through the muddles, mistakes, disappointments, and frustrations, as well as the satisfactions and exultations, of every actual year on an actual farm.

And so it has mattered, undoubtedly it has mattered to my fiction, that I have lived in this place both as a farmer and as a writer. I am not going to pretend here to a judgment or criticism of the writing I have done. I mean only to say something about the pressures and conditions that have been imposed on my writing by my life here as a farmer. Rather than attempt to say what I have done, I will attempt to speak of farming as an influence.

Having settled even in so marginal a place as this, undertaking to live in it even by such marginal farming as I have done, one is abruptly and forcibly removed from easy access to the abstractions of regionalism, politics, economics, and the academic life. To farm is to be placed absolutely. To do the actual work of an actual farm, one must shed the clichés that constitute "The South" or "My Old Kentucky Home" and come to the ground.

One may begin as an agrarian, as some of us to our good fortune have done, but for a farmer agrarianism is not enough. Southern agrarianism is not enough, and neither is Kentucky agrarianism or Henry County agrarianism. None of those can be local enough or particular enough. To live as a farmer, one has to come into the local watershed and the local ecosystem, and deal well or poorly with them. One must encounter directly and feelingly the topography and the soils of one's particular farm, and treat them well or poorly.

If one wishes to farm well, and agrarianism inclines to that wish above all, then one must submit to the unending effort to change one's mind and ways to fit one's farm. This is a hard education, which lasts all one's life, never to be completed, and it almost certainly will involve mistakes. But one does not have to do this alone, or only with one's own small intelligence. Help is available, as one had better hope.

In my farming I have relied most directly on my family and my neighbors, who have helped me much and taught me much. And my thoughts about farming have been founded on a few wonderful books: *Farmers of Forty Centuries* by F. H. King, *An Agricultural Testament* and *The Soil and Health* by Sir Albert Howard, *Tree Crops* by J. Russell Smith, and *A Sand County Almanac* by Aldo Leopold. These writers bring the human economy face to face with ecology, the local landscape, and the farm itself. They teach us to think of the ecological problems and obligations of agriculture, and they do this by seeing in nature the inescapable standard and in natural processes the necessary pattern for any human use of the land. Their thinking has had its finest scientific result thus far in the Natural Systems Agriculture of the Land Institute in Salina, Kansas. Natural Systems Agriculture returns to the classical conception of art as an imitation of nature. But whereas Hamlet saw art as holding a mirror up to nature, and thus in a sense taking its measure, these agricultural thinkers have developed the balancing concept of nature as the inevitable mirror and measure of art.

In addition to books specifically about agriculture and ecology, I have been steadily mindful, as a farmer, of the writers mentioned earlier as literary influences. And I have depended for many years on the writing and the conversation of my friends Gene Logsdon, Maurice Telleen, Wes Jackson, and David Kline. I have been helped immeasurably also by the examples of Amish agriculture, of the traditional farming of Tuscany as I saw it more than forty years ago, of the ancient agricultures of the Peruvian Andes and the deserts of the American Southwest, of the also ancient pastoral landscapes of Devonshire, and of the best farming here at home as I knew it in the 1940s and early '50s, before industrialization broke up the old pattern.

What I have learned as a farmer I have learned also as a writer, and vice versa. I have farmed as a writer and written as a farmer. For the sake of clarity, I wish that this were more divisible or analyzable or subject to generalization than it is. But I am talking about an experience that is resistant to any kind of simplification. It is an experience of what I will go ahead and call complexification. When I am called, as to my astonishment I sometimes am, a devotee of "simplicity" (since I live supposedly as a "simple farmer"), I am obliged to reply that I gave up the simple life when I left New York City in 1964 and came here. In New York, I lived as a passive consumer, supplying nearly all my needs by purchase, whereas here I supply many of my needs from this place by my work (and pleasure) and am responsible besides for the care of the place.

My point is that when one passes from any abstract order, whether that of the consumer economy or Ransom's "Statement of Principles" or a brochure from the Extension Service, to the daily life and work of one's own farm, one passes from a relative simplicity into a complexity that is irreducible except by disaster and ultimately is incomprehensible. It is the complexity of the life of a place uncompromisingly itself, which is at the same time the life of the world, of all Creation. One meets not only the weather and the wildness of the world, but also the limitations of one's knowledge, intelligence, character, and bodily strength. To do this, of course, is to accept the place as an influence.

My further point is that to do this, if one is a writer, is to accept the place and the farming of it as a literary influence. One accepts the place, that is, not just as a circumstance, but as a part of the informing ambience of one's mind and imagination. I don't dare to claim that I know how this "works," but I have no doubt at all that it is true. And I don't mind attempting some speculations on what might be the results.

To begin with, the work of a farmer, or of the sort of farmer I have been, is particularizing work. As farmers themselves never tire of repeating, you can't learn to farm by reading a book. You can't lay out a fence line or shape a plowland or fell a tree or break a colt merely by observing general principles. You can't deal with things merely according to category; you are continually required to consider the distinct individuality of an animal or a tree, or the uniqueness of a place or a situation, and to do so you draw upon a long accumulation of experience, your own and other people's. Moreover, you are always under pressure to explain to somebody (often yourself) exactly what needs to be done. All this calls for an exactly particularizing language. This is the right kind of language for a writer, a language developing, so to speak, from the ground up. It is the right kind of language for anybody, but a lot of our public language now seems to develop downward from a purpose. Usually, the purpose is to mislead, the particulars being selected or invented to suit the purpose; or the particulars dangle loosely and unregarded from the dislocated intellectuality of the universities. This is contrary to honesty and also to practicality.

The ability to speak exactly is intimately related to the ability to know exactly. In any practical work such as farming the penalties for error are sometimes promptly paid, and this is valuable instruction for a writer. A farmer who is a writer will at least call farming tools and creatures by their right names, will be right about the details of work, and may extend the same courtesy to other subjects.

A writer who is a farmer will in addition be apt actually to know some actual country people, and this is a significant advantage. Reading some fiction, and this applies especially to some Southern fiction, one cannot avoid the impression that the writers don't know any country people in particular and are in general afraid of them. They fill the blank, not with anybody they have imagined, but with the rhetorically conjured stereotype of the hick or hill-billy or redneck who is the utter opposite of the young woman with six arms in the picture by the late ("Alas") Emmeline Grang-erford, and perhaps is her son. He comes slouching into the uni-verse with his pistol in one hand, his penis in another, his Bible in another, his bottle in another, his grandpappy's cavalry sword in another, his plug of chewing tobacco in another. This does harm. If you wish to steal farm products or coal or timber from a rural region, you will find it much less troubling to do so if you can believe that the people are too stupid and violent to deserve the things you wish to steal from them. And so purveyors of rural ste-reotypes have served a predatory economy. Two of the Southern Agrarians, I should add, countered this sort of thing with knowl-edge. I am thinking of John Donald Wade's essay "The Life and Death of Cousin Lucius" in *I'll Take My Stand*, and *A Wake for the Living* by Andrew Lytle.

If you understand that what you do as a farmer will be mea-sured inescapably by its effect on the place, and of course on the place's neighborhood of humans and other creatures, then if you are also a writer, you will have to wonder too what will be the effect of your writing on that place. Obviously this is going to be hard for anybody to know, and you yourself may not live long enough to know it, but in your own mind you are going to be using the health of the place as one of the indispensable standards of what you write, thus dissolving the university and "the liter-ary world" as adequate contexts for literature. It also is going to skew your work away from the standard of realism. "How things really are" is one of your concerns, but by no means the only one. You have begun to ask also how things will be, how you want things to be, how things ought to be. You want to know what are the meanings, both temporal and eternal, of the condition of things in this world. "Realism," as Kathleen Raine said, "cannot show us what we are, but only our failure to become that to which the common man and the common woman inadequately, but continually, aspire and strive." If, in other words, you want to write a whole story about whole people—living souls, not "higher animals"—you must reach for a reality which is inaccessible merely to observation or perception but which in addition requires imagination, for imagination knows more than the eye sees, and also inspiration, which you can only hope and pray for. You will find, I think, that this effort involves even a sort of advocacy. Advocacy, as a lot of people will affirm, is dangerous to art, and you must beware the danger, but if you accept the health of the place as a standard, I think the advocacy is going to be present in your work. Hovering over nearly everything I have written is the question of how a human economy might be conducted with reverence, and therefore with due respect and kindness toward everything involved. This, if it ever happens, will be the maturation of American culture.

I have tried (clumsily, I see) to define the places, real and imagined, where I have taken my stand and done my work. I have made the imagined town of Port William, its neighborhood and membership, in an attempt to honor the actual place where I have lived. By means of the imagined place, over the last fifty years, I have learned to see my native landscape and neighborhood as a place unique in the world, a work of God, possessed of an inherent sanctity that mocks any human valuation that can be put upon it. If anything I have written in this place can be taken to countenance the misuse of it, or to excuse anybody for rating the land as "capital" or its human members as "labor" or "resources," my writing would have been better unwritten. And then to hell with any value anybody may find in it "as literature."

# American Imagination and the Civil War

~

## (2007)

Some sentences of the Irish poet Patrick Kavanagh have been prominent in my thoughts for many years:

> Parochialism and provincialism are opposites. The provincial has no mind of his own; he does not trust what his eyes see until he has heard what the metropolis . . . has to say . . . The parochial mentality on the other hand is never in any doubt about the social and artistic validity of his parish.[1]

In spite of necessary qualifications, which I will get to in a minute, Kavanagh's distinction has become indispensable to me in thinking about my native place and history. In Kentucky, a state famously characterized as barefooted, we might oversimplify Kavanagh by saying that those of us who are always admiring our shoes are provincial, whereas the unself-consciously bare or shod are parochial. Or we could more legitimately paraphrase him by saying that people who fear they are provincial are provincial.

I believe I can say truthfully that my particular part of Kentucky, at the time of my growing up in it, was in Kavanagh's terms more parochial than provincial. The parochial in any locality probably always is subject to qualification and inexact in geographical extent. I grew up in a county at that time almost exclusively preoccupied with farming: the county of Henry, a few miles south of the Ohio River. But the country truly native to my family and my experience is in the watersheds of Town Branch of Drennon Creek, Emily's Run, and Cane Run.

During my first twenty or so years, the "social validity" of that place at that time certainly was impaired by racial segregation. That phrase now has the currency of an abstraction, but segregation itself could be experienced only in particular. We were living in the history of segregation, but we were living in it in our place, with our neighbors, and as ourselves. In our small communities segregation involved the wicked prejudice on which it was based, but it also involved much familiarity and many exceptions. Racial inequality was a theory that performed its customary disservices and sometimes justified horrors, but that theory was inevitably qualified by the daily life in which the two races were separate only to an extent. In those places the history of segregation was lived out familiarly by black and white people who knew one another, told stories about one another to one another, helped or harmed one another, liked or disliked one another, and often worked together. Separate and different as the races were, it is impossible to imagine a white person of that place and time whose knowledge did not include the stories, songs, sayings, teachings, and characters of black persons. An honest accounting of the ancestry of my own mind would have to include prominently several black people. Despite segregation, the communities of my young life were, in function and in their consciousness of themselves, more intact than they are now.

❦

As for the "artistic validity" of our place at that time, I have to be both careful and modest. We did have a local music that came to the fore at square dances, though not everybody granted much value to it, and it had begun to be supplanted by music from the radio and jukebox. Most of us were familiar with the Protestant hymns and the King James Bible. But we were not greatly concerned with issues of art, local or otherwise.

The arts that we took for granted, and that did gather us all together, were the arts of farming, gardening, cooking, and talking. Our economy was either agricultural or in service to agriculture. Vegetable gardens, grape arbors, and fruit trees were still commonplace. It was still ordinary to see poultry flocks, fattening hogs, or milkcows in the back yards or back lots of the towns. The grocery stores still bought surplus produce from the farms. Most of the food was homegrown, and excellent cooking was customary. Most of the cooking was done by women, but everybody talked about it.

Everybody, in fact, talked about everything. It seems to me that I grew up totally immersed in talk. Talk was a fifth element: talk in hayfields and tobacco patches, in tobacco barns and stripping rooms, in kitchens and living rooms, on porches and out in the yards. Sometimes, as we sat out in the yard or on the porch after a hot day, the dark would gradually disembody us, and we would become just voices going on until weariness re-embodied us and we would go into the house to bed. My best gift as a writer was that circumstance of talk. We had no cultivated art of conversation. Our talk was practical, local in reference, but was carried on also for pleasure or comfort. It was sometimes crude enough, but it was also articulate enough, humorous, precise, expressive, and sometimes beautifully so.

Though by then most of us had listened to the radio and seen at least a few movies, our talk as yet bore no hint of apology for the way we talked, or for our status as country or small-town people. We knew we were not Yankees, for we had heard Yankees talk and we knew we did not talk like them. We also had listened to people from "down South," and we knew we did not have what we called a "Southern accent." Maybe I can be excused for concluding, when I got old enough to read a map, that I spoke a perfectly average language, Standard American, since I could see that I lived at about the middle of the north–south axis. And maybe I can elicit a little sympathy for my surprise when, having clung to this notion all the way to some literary party in California, I delivered an undoubtedly sophisticated opinion to a literary young lady, whose eyes thereupon grew round with recognition. "Wayull!" she said in Yankee-Southern. "Wheah *you*'all frum, honey chile?"

And so I turned out to be a Southerner—legitimately so, as that term is used. I was born on the south side of the Ohio, was descended from slave-owners, and certainly did not talk like a Yankee.

The problem, as I am hardly the first to know, is that being a Southerner is less a condition than a job. The job, unendingly, is to distinguish between local life and the abstractions that we have allowed to obscure it. There is a huge difference between knowledge and classification. "South" and "Southerner" are not terms that are invariably useful. They belong sometimes to a taxonomy of clichés, stereotypes, and prejudices that have intruded between ourselves and our actual country. These shallow, powerful abstractions have worked to depreciate local knowledge and provincialize local life, and so have denied us the imaginative realizations that alone could have saved our country from the damage that has befallen it.

These old habits of mind and speech have continued in the babbled-to-nonsense polarity of "conservative" and "liberal," and of "red states" and "blue states." This oversimplified language of the media and politics is as far as possible from the best of the local speech I heard as a child, which was like no other in the world because it was of and about our place, which was like no other in the world. In it we were at least beginning to imagine ourselves somewhat as we actually were, and even somewhat as we should have been. Now, under the influence of media speech, we can only pretend and try to be like everybody else.

The problem is that there can be no general or official or sectional or national imagination. The chief instrument of economic and political power now is a commodified speech, wholly compatible with the old clichés, that can distinguish neither general from particular nor false from true. Local life is now a wren's egg brooded by an eagle or a buzzard. As Guy Davenport saw, nothing now exists that is so valuable as whatever theoretically might replace it. Every place must anticipate the approach of the bulldozer. No place is free of the threat implied in such phrases as "economic growth," "job creation," "natural resources," "human capital," "bringing in industry," even "bringing in culture"—as if every place is adequately identified as "the environment" and its people as readily replaceable parts of a machine. Devotion to any particular place now carries always the implication of heartbreak.

I suppose that human minds have always been threatened by the slur and blur of general bias, but it seems to me that this curse fell upon us Americans with a great fatefulness in the circumstances leading to the Civil War, and that the curse has persisted.

The Civil War and the rhetoric associated with it become penetrable by actual thought only when one asks why. Why could people of good sense on both sides not have treated slavery as a problem with a practical solution short of war? The answers, I suppose, are foolishness, fanaticism, sectional loyalty and pride, the wish to protect one's faults from correction by others, moral outrage, self-righteousness, the desire to punish sinners, and sectional hatred.

The Civil War was caused undoubtedly by disagreements over slavery and secession. It was contested so fiercely and so long by the Confederacy undoubtedly because of a truth that our federal government has never learned: People generally don't like to be invaded. But why was there no lenity?

Shakespeare's Henry V, incongruously in the midst of his invasion of France, gives "lenity" a pertinent definition:

> . . . we give express charge that in our marches through the country there be nothing compelled from the villages, nothing taken but paid for, none of the French upbraided or abused in disdainful language; for when lenity and cruelty play for a kingdom, the gentler gamester is the soonest winner.[2]

The word occurs more credibly in Edmund Burke's *Speech On American Taxation*, in which he pleads desperately against the impositions that brought on the American Revolution:

> Yet now, even now, I should confide in the prevailing virtue and efficacious operation of lenity, though working in darkness and in chaos, in the midst of all this unnatural and turbid combination: I should hope it might produce order and beauty in the end.[3]

The American Revolution may have been another "irrepressible conflict," but Burke, who saw it as a civil war, seems never to have doubted that there were two other possibilities: reconciliation on terms of justice or amicable separation.

Lenity can be understood as lenience or gentleness or mercy, and there was too little of it in Burke's England in 1774. There was too little in our North and South from 1861 to 1865, and before, and after. Failing lenity in any conceivable form, relishing its differences, savoring its animosities and divergent patriotisms, the nation divided and went to war. The two sides met in a series of great battles, and at last the strongest won in the name of emancipation and union.

That is the official version, and it is right enough as far as it goes. But to grant a just complexity to this history let us add a third side: that of the dead. Armies, by the necessity and purpose of military organization, are abstractions. We think of battles as convergences not of individuals but of "units." Survivors, in their memoirs, speak as participants. Only in the aftermath of battle, on the nighttime battlefields horribly littered with the dead and the dying, do the individual soldiers begin to enter our imagination in their mere humanity. Imagination gives status in our consciousness and our hearts to a suffering that the statisticians would undoubtedly render in gallons of blood and gallons of tears. Maybe I am speaking only for myself, though I doubt it, when I say that to me the dead in Mathew Brady's photographs don't look like Unionists or Confederates; they look like dead boys, once uniquely themselves, undiminished by whichever half of the national quarrel they died for. In those photographs we meet war as a great maker of personal tragedies, not as a great enterprise of objectives.

Mathew Brady was by no means the first to show us this, nor was Shakespeare, but Shakespeare did show us, with a poignance unsurpassed in my reading, the tragedy specifically of civil war. In *Henry VI, Part III,* there is a battle scene in which first "a Son" and then "a Father," not identified as to side, enter separately, each bearing the body of a dead man whom he has killed and whom he now looks at. The Son says:

Who's this? O God! it is my father's face . . .

And the Father says:

But let me see: is this our foeman's face?
Ah, no, no, no, it is mine only son![4]

Of our own civil war Walt Whitman saw clearly the pageantry and glamour and "all the old mad joy" of battle that Robert E. Lee acknowledged. But he saw also the personal tragedy much as Shakespeare saw it. With the same anonymity as to side, he speaks of coming at dawn upon three of the dead lying covered near a hospital tent:

Curious I halt and silent stand,
Then with light fingers I from the face of the nearest the
   first just lift the blanket;

Who are you elderly man so gaunt and grim, with well-gray'd
    hair, and flesh all sunken about the eyes?
Who are you my dear comrade?

Then to the second I step—and who are you my child and
    darling?
Who are you sweet boy with cheeks yet blooming?

Then to the third—a face nor child nor old, very calm,
    as of beautiful yellow-white ivory;
Young man I think I know you—I think this face is the
    face of the Christ himself,
Dead and divine and brother of all, and here again he lies.[5]

Once dead, the dead in war are conscripted again into abstraction by political leaders and governments, and this is a great moral ugliness. The dead are made hostages of policy to sanctify the acts and intentions of their side: These have died in a holy cause; that they may not have died in vain, more must be killed. And to benefit the victors, there is always the calculation, frequently alluded to but never openly performed: At the cost of so many deaths, so much suffering, so much destruction, so much money or so much debt, we have got what we wanted, and at a fair price.

There is no doubt that wars may have moral purposes. Union and emancipation were moral purposes. So were secession and independence, however muddied by the immoral purpose of slavery. But battles don't have the same purposes as wars. The only purpose of a battle, once joined, is victory. And any price for victory is acceptable to the generals and politicians of the victorious side, who are under great pressure to say that it is acceptable. But the accounting is conventionally not attempted. Victors do not wish to evaluate their victory as a net gain, for fear that it will prove a net loss.

I doubt that such a calculation is possible, even if somebody were willing to try it. But that should not stop us from asking, if only to keep the question open, what we gained, as a people, by the North's expensive victory. My own impression is that the net gain was more modest and more questionable than is customarily said.

The Northern victory did preserve the Union. But despite our nationalist "mystique," our federation of states is a practical condition maintained only by the willing consent of the states and the people. And secession, today, is still not a dead issue. There is now, for instance, a vigorous and strictly principled secession movement in Vermont.

The other large Northern objective, the emancipation of the slaves, also was achieved. But this too appears in retrospect to be an achievement painfully limited. It does not seem unreasonable to say that emancipation was achieved and, almost by the same stroke, botched. The slaves were set free only to remain an exploited people for another hundred years. My guess is that, after the decision was taken to make slavery an issue of war, emancipation was inevitably botched. The North in effect abandoned the ex-slaves to the mercy of its embittered and still dissident former enemy, to whom they would be ever-present reminders, symbols virtually, of defeat.

Furthermore, we have remained a people in need of a racially designated underclass of menial laborers to do the work that the privileged (of whatever race) are too good, too well educated, and too ignorant to do for themselves. Our Stepanfetchits at present are Mexican immigrants, whom we fear for the familiar reasons that we exploit them and that we depend on them.

And so our Civil War raised questions that have been raised a number of times since: Can you force people to change their hearts and minds? Can you make them good by violence? Again and again human nature has replied no. Again and again, ignoring human nature and history, politicians have answered yes. And yet it seems true that Martin Luther King Jr. and his followers, by refusing to answer violence with violence, did more to alter racial attitudes in the South than was done by all the death and damage of the Civil War.

Is this reading of history too idealistic and unforgiving? Probably. Must we not say, pragmatically, that a botched emancipation is better than legal slavery? Well, I am a farmer, therefore a pragmatist: Half a crop beats none; a botched emancipation is better than none. But, as I am a farmer, I am also a critic, and I know the difference between a bad result and a good one. Of our history, though we cannot change it, we must still try for a true accounting. And to me it seems that the resort to violence is the death of imagination. Once the killing has started, lenity and the hope for order and beauty vanish along with causes and aims. Edmund Wilson's logic of the two sea slugs, the larger eating the smaller, then goes into effect: "not virtue but . . . the irrational instinct of an active power organism in the presence of another such organism . . ."[6]

Once opponents become enemies, then the rhetoric of violence prevents them from imagining each other. Or it reduces imagination to powerlessness. Men such as Lincoln and Lee, from what I have read of them, seem not to have been destitute of imagination; of this I take as a sign their grief, their regret for the war even while they fought it. I see them as figures of tragedy, each an instrument of an immense violence which, once begun, was beyond their power to mitigate or stop, and which made of their imagination only a feckless suffering of the suffering of others. Once the violence has started, the outcome must be victory for one side, defeat for the other—with perhaps unending psychological and historical consequences.

When my thoughts circle about, trying to give my disturbance a location that is specific and familiar enough, they light sooner or later on "The Battle Hymn of the Republic." This song has a splendid tune, but the words are perfectly insane. Suppose, if you doubt me, that an adult member of your family said to you, without the music but with the same triumphal conviction, "Mine eyes have seen the glory of the coming of the Lord"—would you not, out of fear and compassion, try to find help? And yet this sectional hymn, by an alchemy obscure to me, seems finally to have given us all—North and South, East and West—a sort of official judgment of our history. It renders our ordeal of civil war into a truly terrifying simplemindedness, in which we can still identify Christ with military power and conflate "the American way of life" with the will of God.

I have made clear, I hope, my failure to perceive the glory of the coming of the Lord in the Civil War and its effects. The North was not uniformly abolitionist; the South was not uniformly proslavery or even prosecession. Theirs was not a conflict of pure good and pure evil. The Civil War was our first great industrial war, which was good for business, like every war since. The Civil War established violence against noncombatants as acceptable military policy. The Army of the United States, no longer the Northern army, proceeded from the liberation of the slaves to racist warfare against the native tribespeople of the West. Moreover, as the historian Donald Worster has said, the Civil War supplanted the "slave power" of the South with the "money power" of the North: "The fact of the matter is we have not even today figured out how to come to terms with the money power that replaced the slave power . . ."[7] The great advantage of the aftermath went, certainly not to the ex-slaves or to the farmers and small tradesmen of either side, not to the people Wallace Stegner called "stickers," but rather to those he called "boomers": the speculators and exploiters, the main-chancers, the Manifest Destinarians, the railroads, the timber and mineral companies.

My purpose in reciting these problems is not to suggest that a Southern victory would have been better—which I doubt—but only to point out that the Northern victory set the tone of overconfidence, of self-righteousness and assumed privilege, that became the political tone of the whole nation.

The Civil War was followed, perhaps as a matter of course—and would have been followed, no matter who won—by the industrial exploitation of our land and people that still continues. While we have stood at our school desks or in our church pews asserting the divine prerogative of "The Battle Hymn," we have been destroying our country. This is not an impression. By measures empirical enough, we have wasted perhaps half of our country's topsoil; we are destroying by "development" thousands of acres every day; we have polluted the atmosphere and the water cycle; we have destroyed or damaged or brought under threat all of our natural ecosystems; in our agriculture and forestry we are treating renewable resources as carelessly as we have burned the fossil fuels; we have severely damaged all of our human communities. We have established unregarding violence as our means of choice in everything from international relations to land use to entertainment.

What are we to conclude? Only, I fear, that violence is its own way, which is entirely unlike the ways of thought or dialogue or work or art or any manner of caretaking. Once you have committed yourself to the way of violence, you can only suffer it through to exhaustion and accept the always unforeseen results.

I have been describing an enormous failure, and to me this appears to be a failure of imagination. Though we are now far advanced in the destruction of our country, we have only begun to imagine it. We are destroying it *because* of our failure to imagine it.

By "imagination" I do not mean the ability to make things up or to make a realistic copy. I mean the ability to make real to oneself the life of one's place or the life of one's enemy—and therein, I believe, is implied imagination in the highest sense. When I use this word I never forget its definitions by Coleridge and Blake, but for present purposes I am going to refer to the writings of William Carlos Williams, whose understanding of imagination, though compatible with that of his English predecessors, is peculiarly American in its urgency.

Three generations and more ago, Williams was fretting about the inclination of Americans to debase their land and, with it, themselves,

> as if the earth under our feet
> were
> an excrement of some sky

and we degraded prisoners
destined
to hunger until we eat filth . . .[8]

We were, he thought, "like a chicken with a broken neck, that aims where it cannot peck and pecks where it cannot aim, which a hog-plenty everywhere prevents from starving to death . . ."[9]

Williams seems to have been one of the few so far who could see the vulnerability of a highly centralized economy. In a letter to James Laughlin on November 28, 1950, he tells of the disruptions of a recent storm, and then he writes:

> But witnessing what one small storm can do to a com-
> munity in these parts I am awonder over the thought
> of what a single small atom bomb might not accom-
> plish. Disruption of every service, now become more
> and more centralized, would starve us out in 3 days . . .[10]

Against such craziness he set the "single force" of imagination: "To refine, to clarify, to intensify that eternal moment in which we alone live . . ." And imagination, in this sense, is not passively holding up a mirror to nature; it is a changing force. It does not produce illusions, or copies of reality, or "plagiarism after nature." And yet it does not produce artificiality. It does not lead away from reality but toward it. It can be used to show relationships. By it "the old facts of history" are "reunited in present passion."[11] Thus I have pieced together Williams' thoughts from the prose fragments of *Spring and All*. Thirty or so years later, in "The Host," one of the devotional poems in *The Desert Music*, he lays it out more plainly, giving it, like Coleridge and Blake, a religious significance:

There is nothing to eat,
   seek it where you will,
      but of the body of the Lord.

The blessed plants
   and the sea, yield it
      to the imagination
intact. And by that force
   it becomes real . . .[12]

If what we see and experience, if our country, does not become real in imagination, then it never can become real to us, and we are forever divided from it. And for Williams, as for Blake, imagination is a particularizing and a local force, native to the ground underfoot. If that ground is not in a great cultural center, but only in a New Jersey suburb, so be it. Imagination is as urgently necessary in Rutherford, New Jersey, or in Knott County, Kentucky, or in Point Coupée Parish, Louisiana, as it is in San Francisco or New York. As I am understanding it, imagination in this high sense shatters the frameworks of realism in the arts and empiricism in the sciences. It does so by placing the world and its creatures within a context of sanctity in which their worth is absolute and incalculable.

The particularizing force of imagination is a force of justice with obvious crucial correspondences in biology and in our legal system. Robert Ulanowicz says that "in ecosystems comprised of hundreds or thousands of distinguishable organisms, one must reckon not just with the occasional unique event, but with *legions* of them. Unique, singular events are occurring all the time, everywhere!"[13] And, except for identical twins, every creature that comes into being by way of sexual reproduction is genetically unique. Recognition of the uniqueness of creatures and events is the reason for the standing we humans grant (when we do grant it) to one another before the law, and it is the reason we "return thanks" (when we do so) for food and other gifts that come to us from the living world. Without imagination there is no right appreciation of these rarities—no lenity, amity, or mercy. And, I think, there is no satisfaction either. Imagination, amply living in a place, brings what we want and what we have ever closer to being the same. It is the power that can save us from the prevailing insinuation that our place, our house, our spouse, and our automobile are not good enough.

Historians and scientists work toward generalizations from their knowledge, just as all of us do. We must do this, for generalization is a part of our means of making sense. But generalization alone, without the countervailing, particularizing power of imagination, is dehumanizing and destructive.

"The South," for example, as the name of an historical side, can have a reckonable and useful meaning. But as the name merely of a part of the country, it means less. If "region" means anything at all, then the South, like the North or the West, is a region of many regions. But so is Kentucky. My county has several distinct regions. My neighbors don't look like Southerners or Kentuckians to me. The better I know them, the more they look like *themselves*. The better I know my place, the less it looks like other places and the more it looks like itself. It is imagination, and only imagination, that can give standing to these distinctions.

If imagination is to have a real worth to us, it needs to have a practical, an *economic*, effect. It needs to establish us in our places with a practical respect for what is there besides ourselves. I think the highest earthly result of imagination is probably local adaptation. If we could learn to belong fully and truly where we live, then we would all finally be native Americans, and we would have an authentic multiculturalism.

And yet the problem I began with has never been resolved: How do we equilibrate or even negotiate between local identity and the abstractions of regional or national identity with the attendant clichés of "economic growth"? Obviously there can be no general answer to this question. If we see the need for an answer, then we must attempt it for ourselves in our communities. I believe that there is hope in the increasing uneasiness of people who see themselves as dispossessed or displaced and therefore as economically powerless. Growing out of this uneasiness, there is now a widespread effort toward local economy, local self-determination, and local adaptation. In this there is the potential of a new growth of imagination, and at last an authentic settlement of our country.

But we must not fool ourselves. This movement toward local adaptation necessarily is being led from the bottom. And it confronts a leadership from the top—in government, in the corporate economy, in the universities—that is utterly lacking in imagination, local loyalty, and local knowledge. Both conservatives and liberals, having accepted the ecological and social damages of industrialism as inevitable, even normal, have conceived the individual as subject alone either to the economy or to the government. In this official numbness, though it is clearly self-doomed, there is for the moment an almost overwhelming power.

Let me give you an example of the way a failure of imagination works against people and land. At present, in the eastern mountains of my state, the coal companies are blasting the tops off the mountains and pushing them into the valleys, covering the streams. They are doing this without concern for the land, the topsoil, the forest, the waterways and the water, or for the homes and lives of the people. This total, permanent destruction is not anomalous in our economy or without causes in our history. I need not delay you here by retelling the history of the corporate pillage of eastern Kentucky, which you will find well told in *Night Comes to the Cumberlands* and other books by Harry M. Caudill, or by describing the culmination of that malignant history in "mountaintop removal," which Erik Reece has accomplished fully in *Lost Mountain*. But if you want to know how this hardly credible or bearable waste could have happened, consider the chapter "Mountain Passes of the Cumberland" in *The Bluegrass Region of Kentucky and Other Kentucky Articles* by James Lane Allen, published in 1892.

Allen was a "genteel" writer of the Bluegrass and an outsider to the mountains, about which he had a curiously divided mind. On the one hand he regarded the then mostly unspoiled forests of that region with a sort of rapture. But he was equally rapturous about the economics and machinery of industrialization. Between these enthusiasms he saw no possible contradiction. The beautiful forest, of course, was invaluable in itself, and it would be nearly completely cut down by the middle of the next century. Beneath the forest lay enormously valuable deposits of coal. Allen accurately foresaw the industrial exploitation of the region, but he thought only good could come of it.

As for the local people, he characterized them in the person of "a faded, pinched, and meager mountain boy" driving a team of oxen and eating from a sack of candy:

In one dirty claw-like hand he grasped a small paper bag, into the open mouth of which he had thrust the other hand . . . He had just bought . . . some sweetmeat of civilization which he was about for the first time to taste.

These people, according to Allen, needed to be civilized and Christianized—which was the official rationale of the federal campaigns against the Indians in the same era.

I don't think Allen was an evil man. Probably, like us, he was pretty good. But he also was ignorant and naive, as we too have been about our continuing bonfire of coal and oil. Being only a prophet, Allen had no doubt about the beneficence of industrialization; he thought it was the coming of the Lord: "You begin with coke and end with Christianity."[14] Compare this bit of prophecy with James Still's *River of Earth*, written half a century later, and you will see what I mean by failure of imagination.

I would like to end by turning to the work of a Southern writer who, for several reasons, is exemplary and dear to me. Ernest J. Gaines inherited the harder side of the racial history that I inherited, and I believe I know some of the questions he faced as he made his way into his work. Could he imagine sympathetically a Southern white person? Could he imagine, so as to require us to imagine, an uneducated black farmhand as a person of dignity, wisdom, and eloquence? Yes, as we know, he could. He has imagined also the community of his people as a part of the life of their place and the hardships of that community. He has imagined the community's belonging to its place, the houses that had the names of people, the flower-planted dooryards, the church, the graveyard, the shared history and experience, the shared stories, the talk of old people on the galleries in the summer evenings and the young people listening. He has imagined also the loss of those things.

In a time when the provincial fear of provinciality has brought the local into suspicion, Ernest Gaines has been true to his place, his people, and their story. He has shown that the local, fully imagined, becomes universal. He has brought his place and his people to such a pitch of realization that again and again as I read him he seems to speak also for me and mine. He has done this in a language like no other, belonging to a place like no other.

His novel *In My Father's House* contains a passage that alarms and consoles me every time I read it. The reason for my alarm is obvious, for the passage is about somebody's damage that becomes everybody's danger. But I consent to the author's understanding of the damage, and I am consoled by the companionship of that.

The main character in the novel, Phillip Martin, gives a ride to a terribly angry young black man named Billy. Billy has been to Vietnam. He is now a would-be revolutionary. He would like to burn the whole country by setting fire to the gasoline in every filling station. In his fury, this Billy is thoroughly frightening. I am frightened of him and for him. But then Billy says:

> You see all them empty fields round here, mister . . .
> Go all over this place—empty fields, empty houses,
> empty roads. Where the people used to be—nothing.
> Machines. Every time they build another machine that
> takes work from the people, they hire another hundred
> cops to keep the people quiet.[15]

And I am caught. I see that Billy and I are joined by a mutual sense of calamity and loss. From my well-wishing in the safety of my chair, I have been carried into the trouble itself that has so nearly consumed Billy. Suddenly, in the midst of his rant, he has spoken from the grief felt by many rural Americans, of whatever race, and certainly by me. I know well that it is possible for me, like Billy, to respond with anger and despair. But I know also that it is possible for me, as for Ernest Gaines, to respond with work, hope, and love.

## Notes

1. Patrick Kavanagh, *Collected Pruse* (London: MacGibbon & Kee, 1967), 282.
2. William Shakespeare, *Henry V*, Act III, scene vi, 111–117.
3. *Selected Writings of Edmund Burke*, ed. Walter J. Bate (New York: Modern Library, 1960), 100.
4. William Shakespeare, *Henry VI, Part III*, Act II, scene v, 61–62, 82–83.
5. Walt Whitman, "A Sight in Camp in the Daybreak Gray and Dim," *Whitman: Poetry and Prose* (New York: Library of America, 1982), 441.
6. Edmund Wilson, *Patriotic Gore*, (New York: Oxford University Press, 1962), xxxii.
7. Chautauqua discussion, 1999 Prairie Festival, the Land Institute, Salina, Kansas.
8. *The Collected Poems of William Carlos Williams, Volume I: 1909–1939*, ed. A. Walton Litz and Christopher MacGowan (New York: New Directions, 1986), 218.
9. William Carlos Williams, *In the American Grain* (New York: New Directions, 1925), 108.
10. *William Carlos Williams and James Laughlin: Selected Letters*, ed. Hugh Witemeyer (New York: W. W. Norton, 1989), 199.
11. *The Collected Poems of William Carlos Williams, Volume I*, 178, 194, 198, 208, 234.
12. *The Collected Poems of William Carlos Williams, Volume II, 1939–1962*, ed. Christopher MacGowan (New York: New Directions, 1988), 260–261.
13. "Naturalism and/or Immanent Divine Action?" Public lecture, Santa Barbara, California, January 26, 2006.
14. James Lane Allen, *The Bluegrass Region of Kentucky and Other Kentucky Articles* (New York: MacMillan, 1900), 277.
15. Ernest J. Gaines, *In My Father's House* (New York: Knopf, 1978), 168.

# The Momentum of Clarity

## (1993)

For a long time, whenever I have thought about Wallace Stegner and his work, I have always come up against the need to make sense of the way influence works within a culture, and my thoughts have always proceeded from that need to a mixture of wonder and confusion. It is nevertheless impossible for me to talk about this man, who for me has been a landmark, without addressing somehow this issue of influence. I will have to address it by way of a little bit of autobiography, and I ask your pardon for this.

I came to Stanford as a fellow in the writing program in the fall of 1958. The seminar in the Jones Room of the library was ably and kindly taught that fall by Richard Scowcroft, and the next spring we continued with Wallace Stegner. Though I remain certain in memory and feeling of the impression this Mr. Stegner made on me, I have a hard time describing it, perhaps because he was not in any sense a "type." He was a fine-looking man of about fifty, gray-haired, courteous, generous, smiling (though perhaps not at something we knew), neatly and even elegantly but never ostentatiously dressed; sometimes, as the class carried on its business of reading and talking, he would smoke meditatively a cigar. He did not seem to be a professor at all, and when he was in it the Jones

Room did not seem part of a school. He had, of course, *been* to school, but one could tell that to a very considerable extent he had not been *made* by school. He managed somehow to imply that the work and the interest that had brought us together were matters in some respects practical. He did not deal in infallible recipes, or guarantee results. He did not suggest that all our problems were solvable. But there was in his presence and bearing the implication that we could work at our problems, and that we should. I thought, and think still, that he was a good teacher. When I sit at my worktable now I am aware of certain attitudes, hesitations, and insistences that I think are traceable to that seminar thirty-five years ago.

I wish I could say that I then understood him as an influence—that I saw what he was about, or saw how to apply his example to my own life. But the fact is that at that time I did not understand him as an influence, and the reason was that at that time I did not know what kind of influence I was going to need. At that time I wanted only to be a writer; beyond that, I had little self-knowledge, and not an inkling of what I wanted to do or where I wanted to do it. I was living outside my life.

I got back inside my life in 1964 when I returned to my own part of the country. From that time I began a long and still continuing process of understanding Wallace Stegner as an influence, and of being influenced by him. But here again I am embarrassed. As I failed to understand him as an influence when I first knew him, so have I failed to know very exactly how his influence has grown upon me; it has been involved in my life as I have lived it.

The difficulty is increased by my inability to separate the influence of the books from the influence of the man himself. Behind the books, for me, has been the presence of a man I would have liked and admired if he had not written a word. And I should add that, to Tanya and me, it has mattered inestimably that he and Mary so obviously and significantly mattered to one another.

Beginning with *A Shooting Star* in 1961, I read Mr. Stegner's books as they came out. In 1962 he published *Wolf Willow*, and I remember clearly my happiness in reading it. With that book, I began to see that side by side with his interest in the West as the subject of his stories and novels was an interest in the West as a place, a living place, *his* living place—and a place, moreover, that had been grossly misunderstood in the course of white settlement and was therefore gravely in need of a complex protection, "a civilization to match its scenery."

Eventually I thought there must have been a moment when he decided that he would not be the kind of writer who would look on his native country as "raw material" for his art, and leave it otherwise to take care of itself or to be cared for by other people, but that he would be a kind of writer who would be devoted to his country for its own sake, and do what he could to protect it. And then I thought that perhaps he had *not* decided—that perhaps there had come a moment, simply, when he realized that he had become that second kind of writer. Whenever and however that moment occurred, it was a significant moment; so far as I know, no American storyteller had been that kind of writer before.

He became the man and the writer he became, of course, because he had entered a web of influence that inclined him to be what he became. The primary influence undoubtedly was his long and intimate knowledge of the country itself, but he acknowledged also the influence of human predecessors. In his conversations with Richard W. Etulain, for example, he said, "Powell taught Webb . . . Powell and Webb, between them, taught Benny DeVoto, and they all taught me." He became an influence, then, partly because he had *accepted* an influence. I entered the same web of influence at a later time and from a different part of the country, but with his work in mind—and when I did finally enter it, Wallace Stegner became my teacher in a way much more profound and useful than before. But "teacher" is not quite the proper word, nor even is "influence" in the usual sense. For he and his work were becoming part of my mind, what I had to think and respond with.

After Edward Abbey died in the spring of 1989, many of his friends met to honor him in the desert near Moab, Utah. Mr. Stegner, who could not attend, sent a letter to be read at the gathering. In it, he said of Ed Abbey, who had been his student, "He was a red hot moment in the conscience of the country." Wallace Stegner also was a moment in the country's conscience—not a red hot moment, but one that was luminous, clarifying, and steady. The word "moment" suggests no dispraise in either case, for these are moments outside of time that can be returned to; the word suggests only that such illuminations occur in a lineage or web of lineages that grows as it continues.

We speak naturally, and I think accurately, of a "web of influence," but it is perhaps useful to change the metaphor by thinking of this influence literally as a flow: a steadily augmenting flow of consciousness and of conscience moving toward our country, the American land itself. One enters into this flow by way of a "moment" (a *momentum*) of clarity instinct with the power to gather other such moments.

It is pleasing and reassuring to remember the care that Mr. Stegner took to understand himself as a part of this still-building influence. As readily as he acknowledged his predecessors, he credited his contemporaries and successors. He was always a giver, never a taker, of credit. In the introduction to his last book of essays, he wrote:

. . . looking at the western writers, not only the ones I will discuss here [John Steinbeck, George R. Stewart, Walter Van Tilburg Clark, and Norman Maclean], but all the new ones, the Ivan Doigs and Bill Kittredges and James Welches, the Gretel Ehrlichs and Rudolfo Anayas and John Daniels, the Scott Momadays and Louise Erdrichs and many more, I feel the surge of the inextinguishable western hope. It is a civilization they are building, a history they are compiling, a way of looking at the world and humanity's place in it. I think they will do it . . . It has already begun.

At first, reading that passage, one may take it to be merely characteristic of his generosity. But then one sees that its governing pronoun is "they": "It is a civilization *they* are building . . . I think *they* will do it." Not many writers, and not many people, have evolved from "I" through "we" to this freely affirmed and welcomed "they." And how moving it is, after looking twice, to see in this almost unnoticeable self-effacement the fineness, the magnanimity, and something of the greatness of Wallace Stegner.

# In Memory: Wallace Stegner, 1909–1993

*~*

## (1993)

Even a week ago, when I knew he was in a Santa Fe hospital, I could have written a tribute to Wallace Stegner more easily than I can now. Then he was alive and I knew exactly what I thought about him, and fairly exactly what I owed him, as a living man. Now that he is dead, I am newly and limitlessly aware of his life and all he accomplished; he is alive still in my thoughts, and is more largely and demandingly present in them than before.

His was an exemplary Western life. He knew the region thoroughly, from the frontier homesteads and settlements of his childhood to its tentatively booming cities of the present day. He had observed it from the perspective of much study and of much travel both in the region and far beyond. He was perhaps his region's greatest teacher: its storyteller, historian, critic, conservator, and loyal citizen. The West, he said, needs "a civilization to match its scenery." His work was all to that end. And because he was so consummately his region's teacher, he was a teacher to us all.

Those who knew him will remember, perhaps first of all, his generosity. For many years, he was head of the writing program at Stanford. He was as useful a teacher in the classroom as elsewhere, conscientious and courteous, modest, unassertively demanding.

And long after he might properly have felt that he was finished with them, his students would know that he was reading what they wrote, mentioning them kindly in his essays, writing recommendations for them, helping out any way he could. He helped other writers who were not his students. His work contains many kindnesses to the lives and works of his predecessors and contemporaries: John Wesley Powell, Bernard DeVoto, John Steinbeck, George R. Stewart, Walter Van Tilburg Clark, and others. And of course there was his long generosity toward the Western land itself, his writings and other efforts on behalf of the causes of conservation. He was no bystander; he served what he cared for. For him, caring and serving were two motions of a single thought.

He was a man of great and rare integrity. He had the look and the bearing of a man willing to make choices, and to stand by the choices he made. He did not condescend or court favor. He did not indulge in that false camaraderie by which one implies that one is "just like" someone else. He was not like anyone else; people were different from one another; he acknowledged this by his reserve, and by a humorous, distant glitter in his eyes. He crossed over his difference from other people many times in his work and in his life, but he would not imply that this crossing was simple or easy, or that it ought to be. His integrity is shown in his work by the care he took to know what he was talking about. Behind everything he wrote is his competent knowledge of history and geography, and his close attention to his own experience.

He was, above all, a writer who knew how to write. He knew exactly what he was talking about, and he put it down exactly as he knew it. In his mastery of his art there is both a proper respect for his subjects and a proper courtesy toward his readers. He played no tricks. He did not exaggerate or sensationalize. He did not display himself. He did not try to get attention by means of shocks or offenses. By the time he got to his last two books—the novel *Crossing to Safety* and the book of essays *Where the Bluebird Sings to the Lemonade Springs*—his work had achieved an astonishing fluency, the ease of almost perfect artistry. He could say directly whatever he needed to say.

It would be possible to go on at length about the beauties and satisfactions of that last book of essays. But to me the most wonderful and by far the most moving essay in that book is the one called "Letter, Much Too Late." It is a letter to his mother, dead fifty-five years, in which he tells her how much he owes her and how much he loves her. It is a settling of an account, an act of justice. But for anyone who knew Wallace Stegner, it is more than that. He was, as he knew and said himself, a reticent man; it was hard for him to say, straight out, what he felt. But in this essay— without, I think, the least diminution of dignity—the reticence is suddenly swept away, and reading the essay is like overhearing a conversation between two souls. For death too is swept away. "Death," he says, "is a convention, a certification to the end of pain . . . not binding upon anyone but the keepers of graveyard records." Death is brushed aside like a hanging cobweb, and the voice of the essay continues out of time, speaking of memories and regrets, calling up visions, telling his mother, with the utmost candor of gratitude and affection, all that he has come to understand, until finally he can say to her as she was, and is, "Any minute now I will hear you singing."

# Speech After Long Silence

— ∿ —

## (1994)

I first heard John Haines read his poems one evening in the Jones Room of the old library at Stanford. That was in 1969, and I still remember clearly the almost incommunicable impression I carried away from that reading. I had heard the poems, the words, but I had also received from them or through them a sense of the condition of mind that had allowed them to be written—though at the time I knew little of the circumstances in which they had been written or the character of the man who had written them.

The explainers of the language of poetry will be forever embarrassed, I hope, by the experience of readers of poetry: Poems tell more than they say. They convey, as if mutely, the condition of the mind that made them, and this is a large part of their meaning and their worth. Mr. Haines' poems, as I heard them that evening, told that they were the work of a mind that had taught itself to be quiet for a long time. His lines were qualified unremittingly by a silence that they came from and were going toward, that they for a moment broke. One felt that the words had come down onto the page one at a time, like slow drops from a dripping eave, making their assured small sounds, the sounds accumulating. The poems seemed to have been made with a patience like that with which rivers freeze or lichens cover stones. Within the condition of long-accepted silence, each line had been acutely listened for, and then acutely listened to.

The poem I remember particularly from that evening is the one called "The Traveler," which speaks of a lamp whose "light came as though from far off / through the yellow skin of a tent," and which ends:

> We were away for a long time.
> The footsteps of a man walking alone
> on the frozen road from Asia
> crunched in the darkness
> and were gone.

Another mystery of reading, or of consciousness itself, is the way an image will return not by intention or even by remembering, but as if by its own power and volition. This image of an anonymous traveler or searcher on a road, since I first heard it, has often returned to me in that way, as apparently it has often returned to the poet, who records it again in "The Forest Without Leaves," a much later poem:

> Snow is falling, the sun is late
> and someone has gone with a lantern
> to search the roads.

And the same image ends his beautiful prose memoir, *The Stars, the Snow, the Fire.*

The attendant silence thus becomes the enabling condition of a kind of language and a kind of knowledge. John Haines homesteaded in Alaska in 1947, when he was twenty-three. He went there, he says,

> To see
> the shadows waver and leap,
> listen to water,
> birds in their sleep,
> the tremor in old men's voices.

Only a few perhaps are able to choose so resolutely such ordinary wonders; Harlan Hubbard of the Ohio Valley was another. This requires a certain constancy and austerity, and an unusual sort of curiosity. One would like to see what the world has to offer more or less on its own—if one will not go too far in search or in pursuit; if one will wait, perhaps for a long time:

> The land gave up its meaning slowly,
> as the sun finds day by day
> a deeper place in the mountain.

And then, finally, one begins to know how "Old ladders shorten, pulled down / in the sod . . ." Or one sees images of travelers, solitary individuals or whole nations, passing over the face of the country, passing over the snow, leaving

> no more sound in the land
> than a handful of berries
> tumbled in a miner's pail

—images that have the power to unite experience, history, and dream, constituting "another episode of the myth-journey of humankind."

The land gives up its meaning slowly, and it is that given-up meaning, patiently waited for, that has moved Mr. Haines' poems, which honor it by a just and frugal speech. How much to his own honor it is that, in an age of easy art, he never has been glib!

Hearing this poet read his poems aloud, or reading them quietly for yourself, you imagine how little "originality" has mattered to him—how little worry he has expended on the latter-day poetical business of "finding his own voice." You must even ask if the voice of the poems is in fact his, and then, when you read *Living Off the Country*, his book of critical essays, you find that the poet himself has addressed this question:

> What counts finally in a work are not novel and interesting things, though these can be important, but the absolutely authentic. I think that there *is* a spirit of place, a presence asking to be expressed; and sometimes when we are lucky as writers, and quiet in a way few of us want to be anymore, a voice enters our own . . .

And he says:

> I have come to feel that there is here in North America a hidden place obscured by what we have built upon it, and that whenever we penetrate the surface of the life around us that place and its spirit can be found.

He therefore speaks of our need for literature "as a matter of practical necessity." And thus his work is far removed from "self-expression" or the "originality" of the personal voice—as is all work that is skilled enough and humbly enough submitted to inspiration.

This, of course, comes of an unabashed love of country—an authentic patriotism—which opens a way beyond our superficial doctrines of self-liberation, self-expression, the modern, and the new. Once a place and its spirit have become not just subjects but standards of a writer's work, then the connections between art and community, art and tradition, art and thought become necessary and clear, and Mr. Haines has been, of understood necessity, a defender of these things. As a critic he has opposed "the cultivation of disorder, the random association of images, the breakup of syntax, the dismissal of intellect, of reason, the continual seeking after 'new thrills' . . ." He has done so, I think, because he opposes the shrinkage of the world to the limits of the isolated, displaced, desiring, and despairing self, the self that ultimately knows nothing and can say nothing:

> you will always be waiting
> for what you do not know,
> knowing that when at last
> it appears you will not know it . . .

How valuable John Haines' work might be to the still preponderant majority for whom the issues of place have been eclipsed by issues of self and career, I cannot say. Of its value, and its potential value, to the increasingly competent minority who long for an authentic settlement of our country, I have no doubt.

# My Friend Hayden

## (2007)

When I was in college and had become certain that Anonymous was not the name of a prolific medieval poet, I began to read the "little magazines" to try to learn about the poetry of my own time. That was in the early fifties. And so I must have known the name Hayden Carruth for a good many years of such scattered reading before it meant much to me.

It began to mean much to me in May of 1964. My family and I had been living as neighbors to Denise Levertov and Mitchell Goodman on Greenwich Street in New York City. Denise and Mitch had bought an old farm in Temple, Maine, where they spent their summers. They invited us to come up for a visit, and in that May we did so. It was a good visit in a good place. The weather was fine, the landscape beautiful, the talk warmhearted. The voice of that time in my memory is that of the white-throated sparrow, who is mostly silent when he winters with us in Kentucky.

While we were there, Denise handed me a sheaf of poems, a carbon copy on yellow paper. The poems were the sequence entitled *North Winter*, by her friend Hayden Carruth. Denise was an ardent and generous friend to the poetry and the poets she liked, and she just as ardently wanted the poets she liked to like each other's poems. She wanted to know if I wouldn't love those poems by Hayden Carruth as much as she did.

To disagree with Denise on such a matter was not invariably cost-free. And so I took the poems in hand with some anxiety, wanting very much to love them as much as she did and very much afraid I wouldn't. But I did, I think, love those poems as much as Denise did. I could see their mastery and their beauty. I could see how entirely the poet loved the place and the creatures he was writing about. Beyond that, those poems were a revelation to me, one I greatly needed at the time.

I was then finishing up two years I had spent in New York, and was about to return to take a job at the University of Kentucky, where, a few years before, I had been a student. Understandably, as I now see, most of my literary friends were upset with me for this choice. They thought I was ruining myself. There I was, with a good job in the great cultural center, getting to know other writers, attending literary events, visiting the museums, in general having a good time—and was I going to turn my back on all that to return to, of all places, Kentucky?

Well, for all I know, they may have been right, for I certainly can't prove them wrong. There are no control plots in one's life. I can't compare the life I've had with the life I might have had. All I can say with certainty, after forty-three years, is that I am glad I chose as I did, I am grateful for the life I have had, and I can see some advantages in living outside the great cultural centers.

But in the spring of 1964 I had not lived the life I was going to live any more than the life I might have lived. I did not, in truth, know what I was doing. I was returning to Kentucky merely because I wanted to; beyond that, I had no reason or argument. And so the admonitions of my friends had affected me strongly.

My first reading of *North Winter* had this context of uncertainty and uneasiness. I did, after all, want to be a writer. I wanted my life to be sustained in part by the intelligence of reading and writing. If I had forestalled or deformed that possibility I would have been diminished, and of course sorry.

I don't think I could have said then why that carbon copy of Hayden's poems meant as much to me as it did. But the poems sank deeply into me, and they consoled me. By now I can say why.

Those poems, in addition to the much else they were, clearly did not come from any great center of culture, not from New York or Boston or even Concord. They came from Johnson, Vermont, a place not central to the culture even of Vermont, and yet a place obviously central to the consciousness and imagination of a fine poet. It was a place that, on the scale of grandeur, might have been any place, except that by the use of his senses, his wits, and his art, the poet had given standing to its unique life, first in his own imagination, then in Denise's, then in mine, and eventually in the imaginations of many others. In those poems I was seeing, though I could not then have said so, the virtue that William Carlos Williams attributed to the work of Poe: a "scrupulous originality, *not* 'originality' in the bastard sense, but in its legitimate sense of solidity which goes back to the ground," a "burst through to expressions of a re-awakened genius of *place*."

The poems of *North Winter* are poems of praise, lamentation, humor, and exuberant technical inventiveness. And they are in a curious way didactic. They are poems of survival. They tell how to be fully and eagerly alive all the way through a cold northern winter.

There is, as Blake rightly said, no competition among true

poets, and I agree, despite the current trade in prizes, grants, and teaching jobs. *North Winter* is not necessarily better or worse than a book of poems from New York or Boston or San Francisco, but it is necessarily different from any book from any of those places or from any other place. It belongs uniquely to the place it came from. But in its fullness of imagination and realization, it belongs also to all of us in our own places. This is not something that one dopes out, or can dope out, by a critical method. It is merely something that one knows, or does not know.

To me, *North Winter* will always speak of the way one poet by his work can help another—or, to put it more truly, of the way a poet by his work can help a fellow human. It told me, at a time when I greatly needed to hear it, that one writer may do life-sustaining work in a place that, to others, would be "nowhere." It told me that somebody rural by predilection, like me, could be a good writer. Soon after I returned to Kentucky *North Winter* was beautifully printed by Carroll Coleman at The Prairie Press in Iowa City. I ordered a copy that I still have and still love, and that still delights and consoles me every time I read it. And so before I became Hayden's friend, I had become his debtor. And my debt to him has steadily grown. I have been mindful of his work and example, and under his influence, for forty-three years.

I became his friend by surprise several years later. On a cloudy afternoon, I was leading a mare and foal from my place in the river valley to my uncle's farm at the top of the hill. A man passed me in a green pickup truck and then stopped up ahead. The man opened the door, stuck his head out, and called, "Are you Wendell Berry?"

I called back, "Yeah!"

"Well," the man said, "I'm Hayden Carruth."

By then I had read more of the poems of Hayden Carruth, and I believe we had written some letters to each other. But I was not prepared to meet him on the road between Lanes Landing and Port Royal. I could hardly have been more surprised if he had told me he was William Shakespeare or Tu Fu. I called back, "The hell you are!"

Hayden stayed with us a night or two on that visit. I showed him around a little, and of course we talked. Our talk, from the first words, was that of friends between whom much does not have to be explained, but rather is assumed or taken for granted. We did not need to tell each other about the happiness of belonging to a place, of loving neighbors who do not read poetry, of ricked firewood, of a garden, of a rough-carpentered shelter for writing, of silence, of the wildness surrounding and suffusing, of handwork outdoors. There are certain griefs and indignations that we have in common also, and have not needed to explain or defend.

We have also understood from the first that Hayden is far better read and better educated than I am. We had to waste no time in settling that. And so I have freely come to Hayden for instruction and correction. And Hayden has freely given the help I have asked for. He has sometimes enjoyed rather extravagantly the authority of his seniority, but then I too have enjoyed it rather extravagantly. There have been moments that have delighted me, and then re-delighted me when I have recounted them to other friends.

Once, for instance, when we were talking on the telephone, I lapsed into the illiteracy I am always tempted to enjoy, and I said something about the need to "lay down" for a nap.

And Hayden said in a split second, "*Lie* down! God damn it!"

That is funny, of course, and I always laugh when I remember it. But it is instructive too. What I took from the instruction, what was instructive about it, was the *force* of it. As it came flying to me through the receiver, I felt and liked and was helped by his unqualified passion for our language and his unrelenting insistence that it should be used well.

Talk is different from writing. Good talk is in some ways better and more precious than any writing. That it goes off "into thin air," leaving a few memories that eventually are reduced to thin air also, in no way detracts from its value. I have been lucky to have a few friends with whom my conversation seems never to resume but merely to continue, and Hayden is one of them.

After Hayden's first visit to Lanes Landing, there have been other visits—never enough, but a good many—at his place and mine, and others, in Pennsylvania and New Jersey, where neither of us was at home except in our long, old conversation.

One fall, maybe not long after Hayden was first here, I visited him at his place, Crow's Mark, near Johnson. We sat and talked in his writing shack, as we had done here in mine, and I helped him put a load of firewood into his woodshed.

Another time I was there in the winter and Hayden took me on my first (and, so far, my only) walk on snowshoes. I had come partly to write an article for *The Draft Horse Journal*, and Hayden drove with me over quite a lot of Vermont and New Hampshire, visiting horse people. I daresay we both remember Anne Harper on a brilliant afternoon running in the snow beside her Belgian stallion, Babar de Wolvertem.

In the summer (I believe) of 1975, Hayden and Rose Marie and their son David visited us here, in weather so much like our own and so little like Vermont's that I was embarrassed. Activity so strenuous as standing still made you sweat through your shirt.

But whatever the circumstances, when we have been together we have talked, and when we have not been together I often have had a book of his poems or essays at hand, and I have read him, as I have listened to him, with respect for his probity, with admiration for his artistry and knowledge, with pleasure, and always with a sense of companionship and consolation.

What I have been trying to prepare myself to say and now will have to say without preparation—for I can see that I am not writing "criticism"—is that, to me, there is an extraordinary continuousness between listening to Hayden and reading him. Some poets seem to me to go to their work as to something removed from themselves, like an office, but Hayden seems to be at his work, or in it, as it seems to be in him, all the time. His poems are not spoken by "the speaker," that suppositional personage of critical convention. When a poem by Hayden is not spoken by a person designated as different from himself, then Hayden is speaking it. When I am talking with him, he is entirely present to me as the poet he is. When I am reading him, I am hearing his voice.

This seamlessness cannot be the result of any sort of idealism. It is the result, I think, of a thought or a hope of a livable life. Hayden's thought, his expectation, starts from and is ever qualified by a careful, deliberate, strictly limited resignation. His work does not arise from a false expectation of ideal causes or effects. He assumes absolutely that our life begins and ends on the everyday, the real, the mortal, the "losing," side of the ideal. In the too-quick view

this may seem pessimistic, but it is never that, or never programmatically that:

> The point is, there's a losing kind of man who still will
> save this world if anybody can save it, who believes . . .
> oh, many things, that horses, say, are fundamentally
> preferable to tractors, that small is more likeable than
> big, and that human beings work better and last longer
> when they're free.

There is a certain darkness in Hayden's affirmation of "the loser,
the forlorn believer, the passer on," but it is nevertheless an affirmation. It is a darkness readily lighted by announcements of great
happiness and great joy.

I think that Hayden's idea of a livable life is a life that has affection in it—a life, to give it the fullest scope of his art, in which
the things you love are properly praised and properly mourned.
What I most value Hayden for and most thank him for (in this
age of deniability, when the merest public honesty is made doc-
trinally tentative) is his wholehearted, unabashed, unapologetic
affection: affection for women and men, for neighbors, friends,
other poets, jazz musicians, wild creatures, beloved places, the
weather. If you know his work, you know you can find dislike in
it, and anger too. Even so, he is a poet of affection. If he dislikes,
that is because he likes. If he is angry, that is because of damage to
what he loves. His affection is capacious and generous; everything
worthy is at home in it. As he knows, everything worthy is frag-
ile and under threat, is prey to time and invisible to power, and
yet affection keeps the accounting in the black. Worthy things,
invested with affection, pass into "the now / which is eternal." I
don't know how this can be, and I don't think Hayden knows.

And yet I believe that it is so; I believe that Hayden believes that it is so.

Affection is the motive force also of his literary essays and reviews, which characteristically are written in tribute to people or work he admires. Maybe therefore he is not a critic, for he doesn't practice the "objectivity" that gives with one hand and takes back with the other and never makes up its mind in favor of anything. And certainly therefore I am not a critic, for I confess that I can't see why anybody would write anything, even the harshest criticism, that doesn't come ultimately from affection. I don't admire poetry that values its subject only as a subject of poetry.

Nobody has been a better servant and teacher of the art of poetry than Hayden has been in his essays and reviews. And there can be no doubt that these have come from his affection, affection that sometimes necessarily requires a passionate discrimination between what is worthy and what is not.

In his essay of 1966, "Ezra Pound and the Great Style," for example, Hayden is carried by his affection for what is best in Pound past the man's obvious faults, with a bare notice that they exist, and straight on to a question of real interest: Why, in spite of all Pound's faults, do we still read him? And Hayden answers: Because Pound's work, preeminently among the poets of our time, reveals "a great and splendid light" that we recognize in all great works of art. And Hayden then devotes his care to that revelation. He speaks of Pound's "vision of the good" ("meaning proportion, plenty, the spirit of the earth at work in man's heart"), and of his belief that "nothing matters but the quality of the affection."

Now I want to consider a poem by Hayden that summons light and vision into the service of affection. The poem is entitled simply "Marshall Washer." It is from Hayden's beautiful book of 1978, *Brothers, I Loved You All*. This poem is immensely important to me—and, I think, to our time—for reasons I hope I can make clear. But I want to write about it now because, in doing so, I may be able to signify my great indebtedness to Hayden and my gratitude.

Marshall Washer was Hayden's neighbor and friend in Johnson, Vermont. They exchanged work and other goods, as rural neighbors once did and now do less and less. On one of my visits to his place, Hayden took me to meet Marshall, who showed me with pride his milking barn and his cows, and with greater pride, because they were his fellow workers, his team of Belgian horses. He was a man I recognized and honored according to his kind (as Hayden had trusted I would do): an excellent farmer and an excellent man. His own generation included many like him on small farms all over the eastern United States. We talked a long time on Marshall's hilltop that afternoon. Our visit included several moments of fine hilarity, courtesy of Marshall's brother-in-law, Wesley, a gifted teller of scandalous tales about himself.

In my copy of Hayden's *Collected Shorter Poems*, I have kept a picture of Hayden in the State House of Vermont on the day in November of 2002 when he was made that state's poet laureate. Standing immediately behind him, wearing a suit and tie, is Marshall Washer. And with that picture I have kept, from the next year, Hayden's eulogy for Marshall, dead at the age of eighty-eight, who "represented, and still does, the finest element of the culture and civilization of northern New England," and who was "the consummate small farmer."

The poem "Marshall Washer" takes up more than six pages in the *Collected Shorter Poems*. It begins with what may seem a sort of wisecrack—"They are cowshit farmers"—but is actually a trap cunningly set, which is sprung about forty lines later, and the snap of it reverberates to the final lines.

The first of the poem's six parts is a small essay on the lives of New England dairy farmers, who sometimes in self-derogation call themselves "cowshit farmers," and whose lives in fact do revolve around the manure that the cows deposit daily in the milking barns and that must be returned to the fields. By their production of milk these farmers make a living. By their handling of the manure they are involved in the fertility cycle, which is the continuity of farming and of the living world. Hayden depends on us to know, as we certainly should, that "manure" means not just excrement but also the handwork and the handcare, by which it is returned to the fields, by which the fields are cultivated, by which, and only by which, we will continue to eat:

> Notice how many times
> I have said "manure"? It is serious business.
> It breaks the farmers' backs. It makes their land.
> It is the link eternal, binding man and beast
> and earth.

"Cowshit," then, has an eternal value. A "cowshit farmer" is an artist whose art makes of cowshit "the link eternal."

The poem then shifts from this description of the kind of man Marshall is to Marshall himself. It is concerned from then on specifically with him—a depiction, an act of understanding and affection, a tribute—though his story clearly also is that of farmers of his kind in the age of industry and urbanization. Part II shows us Marshall at work on his place and in his time:

I see a man notching a cedar post
with a double-blade axe, rolling the post
under his foot in the grass: quick strokes and there
is a ringed groove one inch across, as clean
as if cut with the router blade down at the mill.
I see a man who drags a dead calf or watches
a barn roaring with fire and thirteen heifers
inside, I see his helpless eyes. He has stood
helpless often, of course: when his wife died
from congenital heart disease a few months before
open-heart surgery came to Vermont, when his sons
departed, caring little for the farm because
he had educated them . . .

My quotations by now should have given an idea of the kind of artifact this poem is. Hayden is a poet of extraordinary technical resourcefulness. He is capable of an exacting and refined lyrical beauty. But this poem is built by the gathering in of knowledge. Somewhere not too far in its background are the catalogues of Whitman and their long, accumulating rhythms. But this poem is as far from Whitman's rhetoric as it is from Hayden's own precise lyricism. Its knowledge is more particular, more characterizing, and more exactly compassionate too, than most of Whitman's. The lines of "Marshall Washer" have a certain rough energy that draws specifically personal knowledge into the reach of comprehension and affection. The knowledge is clarified and ordered by the same means that orders the verse: a strictly maintained integrity and clarity of line, a rhythm precisely inflected and perfectly continuous, a sustained impetus of remembrance and reflection that is never overburdened. The lines are not meant to be lyrical, but they are often as prosodically astute as anybody could wish. Look again at that line about manure: "It breaks the farmers' backs. It makes their land."

Because the poem, its language and its prosody, is so nearly at one with its knowledge, it has a quietness that permits accuracy. The poem's story is so fully imagined, is so clearly seen as belonging to its time and place and character, that it can be set down almost casually—"his sons / departed, caring little for the farm because / he had educated them"—though it carries to the heart a mostly unregarded modern tragedy, necessarily personal, but also national and international. That force is not fully released or felt until it is elaborated, with the same quietness of accuracy at the end of the poem:

> No doubt
> Marshall's sorrow is the same as human
> sorrow generally, but there is this
> difference. To live in a doomed city, a doomed
> nation, a doomed world is desolating, and we all,
> all are desolated. But to live on a doomed farm
> is worse. It must be worse. There the exact
> point of connection, gate of conversion, is—
> mind and life. The hilltop farms are going.
>
> . . . . . . . . . . . . . . . . . . . . . . . . .
> the link
> of the manure, that had seemed eternal, is broken.

As you read this poem, a terrible beauty leaps from it into your consciousness—if your consciousness has been at all prepared to receive it. The terribleness is in the story of the breaking of "the link / of the manure"—the work and the care, the fertility cycle in agriculture—which "seemed eternal" perhaps because it was, and because it was, and is, necessary if survival is to be a part of our intention. The beauty is in the verse, which is to say in the poet's enactment in verse-making of his intelligent love and regard for Marshall Washer.

Marshall's farming, by which he maintained "the link eternal" of the manure, we must see as an enactment of reverence. And here it is necessary to distinguish the reverence that is enacted from that which is merely felt. Our survival, our culture, and our civilization, if they are to be even worthy of survival, depend on our ability to supply to the feeling of reverence the arts necessary for its enactment. Poetry and farming have to be counted equally as two of the necessary arts; and we must understand at last that Hayden's poem is an appreciation of one fine artist by another: reverent men, both of them.

I am a reverent man myself, a farmer and a poet, and I am therefore party to this poem of Hayden's about his friend Marshall Washer, as I was one afternoon, by Hayden's hospitality, party to their friendship and conversation. I am party, moreover, to their fate as rural people. When I read *North Winter* for the first time I was on my way back to my own rural place and life. But I was also going back, as I half knew even then, as I know more completely now, to take up the fate of country people in my time. I was going back to help bury a lot of good men and women who had replaced their predecessors well enough, but who themselves would not be succeeded or replaced. I was going back to witness many times the breaking of the old link and the old reverence of the manuring of the fields.

Near the end of his essay on Ezra Pound that I quoted earlier, Hayden wrote:

How shall our children live in a world from which first the spirit, then history, and finally nature have fled, leaving only the mindless mechanics of process and chance: Will any place exist for a humane art in a society from which the last trace of reverence—any reverence—has been rubbed out? As a matter of fact I think a place will exist, will be made . . .

Hayden wrote those sentences more than forty years ago, and yet when I read them now, in spite of the troubles and discouragements of those years, I still feel spoken for. It is the right thought, the right faith, whatever happens.

Can modern Americans conceive of a reverence for "the eternal link" of manure? Well, Hayden can, and I can. And I could quickly fill this page with the names of people I didn't know forty years ago, people in America and in other countries, who can conceive of such reverence, who in various ways practice it, and who could fill pages of their own with the names of others who do—a cowshit sodality making places for reverence, still faithful to the old linkage, its knowledge and its work.

## Postscript

Hayden died (as we so crudely say) on September 29, 2008, at 9:08 in the evening. I wrote a memorial piece about him for *The Sewanee Review*, from which I will add the following paragraphs in memoriam:

Nobody's life is easy. Hayden's life, in some ways, may have been more than ordinarily difficult. In addition to the expectable hardships and griefs, he had mental problems, a problem with alcohol, and for many years he made a marginal and uncertain living as a literary handyman, editing, reviewing, and odd-jobbing. He wrote his share of complaints, but his complaints were about realities. In facing hardships, those that were generally human and those that were peculiarly his own, Hayden was unflinching.

But his complaints were not *merely* complaints. I think Yeats said (or if he didn't he should have) that we don't value literary works solely because of the pain in them. That may sound cruel, but it is true. It is a truth disregarded by the writers of our day who apparently think their realism is authenticated only by their fixation on misery, violence, ugliness, and despair. I keep coming upon books (and avoiding books, having been forewarned by reviews) whose authors follow the medical establishment in regarding death as a cosmic error and a personal affront, at the same time finding life to be insupportably painful, at the same time ducking their logical obligation to shoot themselves. Why should one read a book that is programmatically more depressing than the news?

Hayden wrote no more painful poem—I know no more painful poem—than "Dearest M—," a poem on the first day after the death, from cancer, of his only daughter Martha. This is a poem that should not be sampled, and so I won't quote parts of it. The poem describes Martha, tells her story, praises her, grieves over her, and struggles, sometimes violently, with its inevitable failure to deal adequately with the enormous facts of her suffering and her absence.

The poem is a protest against the death of Martha, but it is much more than a protest. Its sorrow is never the self-centered, self-indulging sorrow of our woe-wallowing realists. The poem is harrowing, and yet there is nothing of denial or negativity in it. It is, in the hardest way, an affirmation. Its grief is understood throughout as a part of praise and a sign of love. There is a stark wit in the poem's steadfast resistance against the curve of the classical elegy, which ends in comfort, waving the departed soul into Heaven and wiping away tears. This poem pointedly sheds no tears, and just as pointedly it refuses comfort. One recognizes Hayden's crankiness and stubbornness in this, but that stark and unrelenting wit is in it also. He will not even suggest, with Ben Jonson and others, that too much affection for a mortal child may be a mistake. To do so would be self-indulgent. By refusing comfort he keeps his love intact and remains true to it.

In a time so "realistically" focused upon pain, it seems too likely that this poem will be valued only for its pain—or that readers will see only pain in it. I speak of it here, not only for its obvious deserving, but also to recognize the great praise and love that are in it. It is important to see that Hayden does not falsify or flinch from the world's suffering, but it is no less important to know that he is a poet of love and praise.

His friends know him also, both poet and man, as a fine companion, a man of passionate allegiances and affections, and a splendid laugher. Reading him, as in his company, you commiserate, but you also laugh.

On his first visit here Hayden told me at length about an exchange of letters in his local newspaper on the question of the production of split peas for split-pea soup. Many ingenious techniques and technologies were brought forth, until Hayden put an end to the discussion by coming up with the obvious solution: the least laborious method of split-pea production is to *plant* split peas. Our friend David Budbill tells me that Hayden further pointed out that if you will plant a hambone with your split peas, your pea hulls will be full of split-pea soup ready-made.

This is the frontier humor of Mark Twain and others, which tells an elaborate, obvious falsehood straight-faced as the truth.

And so I offer "Crow's Mark" as one of Hayden's poems that I would most like him to be known by. The poem is mostly a matter-of-fact geography of his home place at Johnson, Vermont, which lies "in the bottom of Foote Brook Gulf," "gulf" being the local word for the valley of a small stream. There is a discussion of the topography, the brook, the prevailing wind, and then we have this:

>                           sometimes,
> usually ten or twelve nights a winter,
> the wind veers round due north, straight
> down from the pole, and when it hits the Gulf
> it's like full-choke on a twelve-gauge
> barrel—compression, you know what I mean?
> I mind one time
> in January—'sixty-eight, I think it was—
> the wind blew the beam of my flashlight
> twice around the maple by the woodshed
> and wrapped it tight. You don't
> believe me? Ask Marshall. The flashlight
> was hanging there still next morning.
> I let it stay till the batteries wore out
> and it fell down.

# In Memory: James Still

## (1997)

In the summer of 1954, I believe it was, I borrowed my father's car and went up to a writers' conference at Morehead State College in Morehead, Kentucky. I was a boy of about twenty, who had heard of the literary world and wished to meet it face to face. The literary world exists, of course, only at a distance. At Morehead, I met face to face a writer named James Still, by birth a native of Lafayette, Alabama, but who had become (and has remained) by work, knowledge, and devotion a native of Knott County, Kentucky.

That meeting has stayed extraordinarily clear in my memory—not, probably, because of Mr. Still's impeccable courtesy and kindness in talking about my little piece of apprentice work, but rather because of the advice he gave me. The advice was stunningly—and, I now think, brilliantly—practical. He leapt right over the issues I undoubtedly expected him to deal with—talent, perception, the art of writing, publication—to the issue of work. Writers, he told me, needed to work, and to work they needed time. Time was the problem. When, for example, he was employed as a librarian, he found it necessary to get up *early* in the morning, before the world began its schedule. He sat down then in the quiet and worked at his writing.

I have now thought about that advice for forty-three years, and I do not see how it could have been better. Ordinary teachers, it seems to me, always try to set a young person on the right path. Mr. Still, whom I count as an extraordinary teacher, took the path for granted, and led me straight to what he had found to be the most difficult obstacle. He thus implied a question: How serious are you? And he then, without presumption, gave me to understand that, to the extent that he had dealt with the problem of work and time, *he* was serious.

In the years that followed I remembered his advice about capturing time and benefited from it. More important, what he said caused me to imagine him as a writer. That I imagined what I never saw probably means that I did not imagine him as he actually was, and perhaps that does not matter. It has, however, mattered greatly to me that ever since that brief meeting I have always had in mind, and particularly as I have read and reread James Still, that quick-caught imaginary glimpse of a man quietly serious rising early and sitting down to work in the dark of the morning.

Over the years, my understanding of his writing, and of writing in general, has grown as a result of my effort to know what he was doing in those hours that he used for his most solitary and necessary work. I can say only that I know a little: I know that he was imagining something and putting it down so skillfully in words that whoever read them could not help but imagine the same thing; I know that to do this, he was employing talent, perception, and art, and was probably ignoring or forgetting the issue of publication. I know that, for him as for the rest of us, the life and conviviality of imagined things finally has depended upon the small acts and judgments of art, which is to say upon work—which is what, I think, he was telling me in 1954.

But about here we enter mystery. I really don't know how he

has done what he has done, and finally I must understand his work just by admiring it. I think that up there in Knott County, well off the main track of the literary world, he became a nearly perfect writer. His stories consist of one flawless sentence after another. The words are rightly chosen; the rhythm is right; the sentence is rightly poised within the paragraph and within the story as a whole. I admire his short stories and his novel *River of Earth* for their concentration and movement. Every word moves the story. Nowhere does one find the extraneous or superficial detail that requires hesitation and means distraction. The stories have both economy and amplitude; they make of economy the very instrument of amplitude. Not many writers ever have been able to concentrate so much power into a few pages. When you look up from "The Nest" or "The Scrape," you find the room filled with afterimages, and you must sit awhile before you can think of something else. Because, I think, of its artistic integrity, this body of work never exploits or condescends to its subject, a region that has been condescended to and exploited almost by convention.

Mr. Still's poems have the same thriftiness and concentration as his prose. They are more personal, in the sense that in them he is more obviously speaking for himself. They are the work of a man accomplished in gentleness, humorousness, compassion, and clarity. Some of his poems, because of occasions on which Mr. Still has read them, have become communal works, and have had meaning added to them, so to speak, after the fact. I, for one, will not forget his reading of the poem "Heritage" at the funeral of Harry Caudill.

Thus, by his work, his teaching, and his example, for a long time, James Still has been showing us how precious things are preserved and cultures made.

# A Master Language

~

## (2001)

If one believes as I do that James Still is a master of the short story—one who in execution is virtually flawless, in touch and ear so nearly perfect that the difference does not matter—then one must ask why this is not more generally recognized. This may seem easily explained by prejudice against country people and country things, whatever is perceived as regional or local, and yet in Mr. Still's lifetime a number of other rural writers rose to favor with both critics and the reading public.

The problem, more likely, is his reliance on the native dialect of the Kentucky mountains (perhaps he would prefer to say the native dialect of Knott County) which always informs the language of his stories. And so any assessment of his work must begin with an examination of his language.

Mr. Still gave his whole attention to a people who not only are regional, rural, and "backward," but who until fairly recently spoke a regional dialect that was intact and vigorous; it had the accuracy and expressiveness of a common language rising out of common experience. To present-day Americans, whose speech always contains a deference to the jargon, the invented dialects, of specialists and experts, the language of Mr. Still's characters must seem to come from another world—which it does.

But the critical question is not whether or not a writer uses a dialect, or whether or not the dialect is old or obsolete, but whether or not that dialect has benefits to confer on the writer who uses it, and whether or not the writer has benefited. Mr. Still's short stories give proof that the dialect of his people had plenty of benefits to confer, and that he benefited plentifully.

It is evidently tempting, when speaking of this body of work, to carry it into the neighborhood of words such as "folk," "primitive," "archaic," and "Americana." Thus an incoherent culture condescends to a coherent one, and in the process overlooks the artistry of James Still, whose work claims our interest not as a display of folk speech or folk knowledge, but because of his superb storytelling, the richness and subtlety of his understanding of character, and his extraordinary clarity of feeling.

Mr. Still's language is not that of "local color" or "regionalism." It is not "realistic" or "picturesque" or "quaint." It involves no condescension to the local. By it, simply, he gives his prose the economy, liveliness, and density of poetry. The speech of his characters is elegant, and it is eloquent. It is certainly not an obstacle to get over in order to learn the story, any more than is the language of Chaucer or Shakespeare. The story is in the language in which it is told, and nowhere else.

Searching for a way to take this work as seriously as I believe it deserves to be taken, I came upon this: "He had got emotion, the driving force he needed, from his life among the people, and it was the working in dialect that had set free his style." That is from Lady Gregory's essay on John Millington Synge in *Our Irish Theatre*. And turning to Synge himself, I found the following in his preface to *The Playboy of the Western World*: "in countries where the imagination of the people, and the language they use, is rich and living, it is possible for a writer to be rich and copious in his words, and at the same time to give the reality, which is the root of all poetry, in a comprehensive and natural form . . . On the stage one must have reality, and one must have joy . . ."

Laying aside the difference that Synge's "life among the people" was sadly shorter than Mr. Still's, it is useful to think of the several likenesses between these two lives and bodies of work. Both men went to live among the people they wrote about. In the work of both you feel, behind the presence of the writer, the presence of a solitary, endlessly patient listener and observer. And in both you apprehend an intense, uncompromising artistry. Neither of them offered as dialogue the raw chatter that writers use when they want to show off their provincial characters to urban readers. The language of each is in no sense merely "found" but is a splendid artifice. The dialect is not used for any form of display, but for what it lends of energy, particularity, metaphorical richness, wit, economy, and swiftness. Every speech reveals character and moves the story forward.

It is the energy and richness of Mr. Still's language that permit him to enter right into the story with no more scene setting and character description than if he were Shakespeare. By this language, in which the community speaks along with the individual, even a small girl or boy, in speaking, is surrounded with a distinctive landscape and culture.

Mr. Still's stories give us the reality that Synge called for, and the joy as well, but they do not accomplish this by what is called realism. There is, of course, a difference between realism and what Synge called "reality." Realism is the most fraudulent of literary illusions because it promotes in its theory the illusion that it is not an illusion. "Reality" in art is life made immediate to the imagination. Like Synge's plays, Mr. Still's stories feed on observation and hearsay, but they give us, not what has been seen and heard, but what has been imagined. The story set before us moves us because it is imaginable as lived life; its language is imaginable as spoken speech. We do not read as observers of putatively "real" events that have been observed, but rather as participants in events that have been so fully imagined that we too cannot help but imagine them.

Nothing that I have said takes away from the fact that these stories can be read as "a social diagram of folk society such as hardly exists today," as Mr. Still himself once said. They are that—though I am more and more inclined to distrust the word "folk." That we can learn from them about a society that no longer exists is a part of their value, as it is part of the value of Homer or Jane Austen. But it is also true that, as the writer of these stories, Mr. Still was never a collector or a researcher—not a sociologist or a folklorist or an anthropologist. We will continue to read them, and to want to read them, because they were written by a surpassing artist.

There is no way to separate the issue of language from the issue of subject. That Mr. Still's characters, who speak a dialect now hardly heard, are members of a society that now hardly exists may be one more reason why some readers would like to classify them as exhibits of "Americana" or "folklore." Mr. Still began to know these people in 1932, when their traditional ways were already under extreme pressure from the industrial economy imposed on their region by the coal companies. One of the themes of his work is the tension felt in families between the opposite pulls of their old agrarian life and of employment, however undependable, in the mines. The old life had not yet died; it was still present, still observable, its outline clarified perhaps by its passing away, and in some of his stories Mr. Still seems to be reaching toward it, attempting to see it whole in his imagination.

But as with dialect, the critical question about "folk society" as a subject is not whether or not it is used, but whether or not it is useful. What does it have to offer? To Mr. Still his experience of the doomed traditional society of the Kentucky mountains offered, I believe, not archaism but coherence, not Americana but a vision of life lived elementally. The coherence of culture provided for a coherence of character, perception, and event such as the world will not soon know again. A writer, writing about such a culture, is invited to see it whole, as it sees itself. He will see its tragedy and its comedy, its pathos, meanness, and cruelty, its kindness and its beauty, and he will see each of these compassionately and humorously, without looking away from the others.

It is tempting at this point to begin a description of the various stories, speaking of the delicacy of "Mrs. Razor," the pity and terror of "The Nest," or the outright horror of "The Scrape." But readers can read the stories, which is better than reading descriptions of them. I would like to speak instead of the instructiveness that arises from a certain difference between our own present society and that earlier "folk society such as hardly exists today." The difference is that certain matters that were merely personal or communal in the old society have now become ferociously political.

Kentucky's one-room schools have always been held up as symbols of backwardness and deprivation. But I could not help but notice, in reading again Mr. Still's stories of mountain schools, how permeable was the boundary, for better and for worse, between community and school. The state educational bureaucracy was remote, and the school was the community's concern—two facts that are undoubtedly related. This is nowhere the point of Mr. Still's stories, but is observable in them.

And I could not help wondering what modern feminists and antifeminists would make of "A Master Time," in which there is sexuality and sexual contention but no sexual politics. (Where there is no thought of a "public," the private cannot become political.) An unnamed storyteller, evidently a bachelor and something of an outsider, is invited to a hog-killing which is also an all-day and overnight social event. The company is made up of six young married couples, the storyteller, and an ancient midwife, Aunt Besh Lipscomb. The work of the hog-killing is accomplished, there is a great deal of cooking and eating, the women laughing in the kitchen while the men eat, and there is—for the men—a churn of good whiskey in the smokehouse.

Perhaps because of the whiskey, a little estrangement begins and grows between the husbands and the wives. It is carried on in jokes and laughter, but it is there, it is finally strong, and it is resolved deliciously, and convincingly too, in a snowball fight! This is very much a story of individual people, but it is also a sort of ritual drama in which the community first expresses and then dissipates an old discord that it knows will go on interminably. There is a residual bitterness in Aunt Besh, whose trade, after all, has been childbirth and suffering, and who is partial both to the young wives and to the whiskey. "Kill 'em," she cries to the women during the snowball fight. And at the end, finding that the churn is empty, she says, "I'll endure." So must the young couples, and bitterness will not help them much. That is why their reconciliation has an emotional charge that carries us far beyond the hilarity of its means.

This story is absolutely lovely, quick and alight with shifting tones. It is a little globe, a world called into existence, reality, and joy, by a master workman.

# My Conversation with Gurney Norman

## (2005)

I have been reading again my notes from a trip I made to see Gurney Norman in mid-July of 1965—forty years ago. Gurney was living then in Hazard, Kentucky, working for *The Hazard Herald*. I had known him for about nine years.

We first met when we were both students at the University of Kentucky in the spring of 1956, when I was a senior and Gurney was a freshman. I had taken part, one afternoon, in an English Club panel discussion of the work of T. S. Eliot, a subject on which I was perfectly unqualified to speak in public. At the end of the meeting, this young student with a bur haircut, wearing an Army ROTC uniform, came up to me and said something like, "Now tell me more about this poet T. S. Eliot."

I remember that encounter probably because of my embarrassment, for I had already said all I knew about T. S. Eliot, plus some more. It would have been gratifying to respond to Gurney's misplaced confidence with real erudition. I don't remember what I said, but I hope it wasn't much.

After that, I eventually learned from our mutual teacher and friend Robert Hazel that Gurney was a promising writer; I read (and still remember) one of his early stories in the campus magazine *Stylus*; and in various encounters we got to know each other a little. We wrote a few letters back and forth, and in the spring of 1964, when my family and I were returning from New York to Kentucky, we stopped at Gurney's house in Hazard and spent the night.

But our actual friendship, which is to say our actual conversation, began with that July trip of mine in 1965. I drove up to Hazard on the fifteenth, a Thursday, got there in the middle of the afternoon, and found Gurney at work in *The Hazard Herald* office. He showed me around, gave me a quick lesson in typesetting, and sent me off to read and take a nap while he finished his day's work.

That night we attended a tent revival that was a wonder of its kind. The next day and the next we drove the mountain roads and backroads; we looked and talked. When we needed to, we stopped the car and got out and looked closer and longer, and then we drove on, still talking. We went to Four Seam and Big Creek, to Chester Cornett's place on Troublesome Creek near Dwarf, to Bulan, Hardburley, Clear Creek, Hindman, and Whitesburg.

On the mountain above Hardburley we stood and looked at the first working strip mine I ever saw. It had never occurred to me that people could destroy land with an indifference that perfectly matched the capability of their technology. The big machines were following the seam of coal around the mountain, leaving a high vertical wall like an open sore on one side and on the other the "overburden" of earth and rock thrown regardlessly down upon the forest and the streams below.

We drove through valleys where human life had grown careless and halfhearted under the influence of the coal industry and its invariable ruination. We drove through other valleys spared so far the misfortune of coal, where the modest houses were painted and there were flowers in the dooryards and excellent vegetable gardens.

On the day I arrived, as it happened, a brave old man, Dan Gibson, had gone onto a strip mine that was threatening his grandson's land. The grandson was at that time serving in Vietnam, protecting from communism the right of the coal companies to ravage his homeland under the then-prevailing broad form deed. Dan Gibson had turned the bulldozers back with a squirrel rifle, he being past eighty, he said, and having nothing to lose by dying. He had then been arrested by thirteen state police, a sheriff, and two deputies, jailed, and then released under a $2,000 bond.

In response to that episode there was a meeting of the Appalachian Group to Save the Land and the People in the courthouse at Hindman on Friday night. Gurney and I went to the meeting, where he introduced me to Harry and Anne Caudill. We listened as Leroy Martin, spokesman for the Group, told the story of Dan Gibson's heroism and his arrest. And then we heard Harry Caudill make a great talk in which he spoke of "the gleeful yahoos who are destroying the world and the mindless oafs who abet them."

On Saturday we walked a path up a mountainside to see the Ritchie family's small house that had been shoved down the mountainside by the sliding "spoil" off a strip mine. We talked a long time with Harry Caudill over lunch in a restaurant in Whitesburg, and we went to see Tom Gish, editor of *The Mountain Eagle*, whom I met then for the first time.

Those days and nights, as I said, were the real beginning of my conversation with Gurney. And that conversation, though many times interrupted, has not stopped in the forty years since. We have traveled many other days and nights in eastern Kentucky, Gurney always serving as my faithful guide and interpreter, my Virgil, telling me what to see and what it meant, telling me the stories, *his* stories, that belong to the places we have gone—as I suppose I have served as his Virgil down here at the lower end, which is my end, of the Kentucky River.

The axis of our conversation has been this river. Its headwaters gave Gurney his formative experience and have kept his allegiance and attracted his thoughts all his life. My own life was formed and has been lived mostly down here near the mouth. We have spoken to each other from opposite ends of this gathering of water, I speaking upstream to Gurney, he downstream to me. We have driven the roads and walked the paths, telling each other our stories, sending up our laughter like a ceremonial smoke. Some stories we have told again and again, trying to tell them right and to have them rightly understood. The effect has been stereoscopic.

What has this conversation been worth? Well, try imagining an upstream or a downstream writer traveling alone, talking to himself.

# Sweetness Preserved

(1998)

What I am going to do is talk about some poems—lyric poems—as the products of a story. Most poems, whether or not they tell or contain stories, come out of stories, and often they bear reference to the stories they come out of. For a couple of generations now, critics and teachers have not thought it wise to approach poems by way of stories. They have thought that poems should be read "as poems" or "as texts," as words written or printed on a page, ignoring the story the poems come out of.

I am willing to suppose (for the sake of supposing) that such poems as I am going to talk about must finally shrug off their stories, and all else they do not explicitly contain, and stand before us on their own. I am aware that some poems stand before us on their own because they must; we do not know the stories they came from. But in reading poems that are perfectly anonymous, we still know that there is more to them than the "text." We think of a poem and in the same thought think of what it is about, if it is about anything. Literature involves more than literature, or we would not be grateful for it.

Suppose we know not only a body of poetry but also the story that the poetry came out of. How then are we to help knowing what we know? How are we to help knowing, for instance, that some poets are pilgrims, and that their poems are not just objets d'art, but records, reports, road signs, or trail markers? By what curious privilege are we allowed to ignore what we know?

But I would like to go a little further still, and honor the possibility that the stories that poems come out of are valuable in themselves, so far as they are known. Those who are living and writing at a given time are not isolated poetry dispensers more or less equivalent to soft-drink machines, awaiting the small change of critical approval. We are, figuratively at least, members of a community, joined together by our stories. We are inevitably collaborators. We are never in any simple sense the authors of our own work. The body of work we make for ourselves in our time is only remotely a matter of literary history. The work we make is the work we are living by, and not in the hope of making literary history, but in the hope of using, correcting so far as we are able, and passing on the art of human life, of human flourishing, which includes the arts of reading and writing poetry.

There is a danger of presumption or imposition in what I am about to do, for I am not an authority on the story I am going to talk about. The story of a person's life cannot be entirely known or told. However, I do know unavoidably and unforgettably that Jane Kenyon's poems came out of a story. I know as well that Donald Hall's did. And I know that the poems of both poets came to a considerable extent out of the same story—or perhaps out of the intersection or overlapping of two stories; I want my language to be accurate and courteous, and am not confident of my ability to make it so.

The story of Donald Hall and Jane Kenyon is not my story. And yet their story is not absolutely distinct from mine, for their story is one I have depended on, and have spent a good deal of

time telling over to myself and thinking about. And I have been
attentive to the poems that came out of it. Their story and their
poems have affected, instructed, troubled, consoled, and clarified
my understanding of my own story.

Because I am a storyteller and was from childhood a hearer and
reader (and believer) of stories, I have always known that people
live in stories. And so it has been a little shocking to me to realize
also that it is possible for people to wander outside their stories.
When Donald Hall and I first met, at a literary party in Manhat-
tan in the winter of 1963, both of us were living outside our stories.
I find it readily supposable that Don didn't know what to make of
me, even if it is supposable that he tried to make anything of me
at all. I certainly didn't know what to make of him, and the reason
was that I didn't know what to make of anything. Later, when
both of us were again living inside our stories, we would recognize
each other and become friends. This happened, I think, because
we both loved our grandparents and we both derived from childhood homeplaces that we did not like to forsake. We have corre-
sponded in two ways.

At the time of the party in 1963, the two of us were in "exile."
I give that word an emphasis because it was so important and
applied so peculiarly to young writers in our generation. We came
to our calling in the shadow (and the glamour) of eminent literary
exiles: James, Pound, Eliot, Joyce, Stein, Hemingway, and others.
Moreover, those in charge of our education tended to think that
they were preparing us for careers, not for settling down some-
place. The question before us seemed to be, not how we might fit
ourselves and our book knowledge into our home landscapes, but
how we would fit into our careers, which is to say our exile.

This is confirmed by Donald Hall's early poem entitled "Exile."
Looking back at that poem now, I find nothing in it that surprises

me. It is a good poem. It is also an inevitable product of the poet's era and education; it *had* to be written by somebody. It states the case beautifully:

> Imagining, by exile kept from fact,
> We build of distance mental rock and tree,
> And make of memory creative act . . .

This is an exact enough description of the poet's job of work in Don's "Elegy for Wesley Wells," also an early poem. It too is a good poem—I don't mean at all to be denigrating this work of "exile." In the elegy, the poet mourns and celebrates his grandfather Wesley Wells, a New Hampshire farmer, a good one apparently, but one belonging to an age that, at the time of the poem, is "bygone." The poet (in the way of a young elegist, which I was once myself) is hoping to grant a measure of immortality to his grandfather by means of his poem. It is, to me, an extraordinarily moving poem. I have never read it without being moved by it, though by now I have lived beyond the notion that immortality can be conferred by a poem, and though by now my reading of the poem is influenced by my knowledge of a story that the poem, so to speak, does not know. When I read "Elegy for Wesley Wells" now, I feel a humorousness and a sadness that the poem did not anticipate.

In immortalizing his grandfather Wells, Donald Hall the young elegist is also immortalizing a part of his own life which he now considers to be finished. That life, if it is to have a present life, must have the immortal life of art. Maybe you are outside your life when you think your past has ended. Maybe you are outside your life when you think you are outside it. I don't know what Donald Hall in later life would say. I know only what I in later life would say. I would say, partly from knowing the story I am talking about, that though you may get a new life, you can't get a new past. You don't get to leave your story. If you leave your story, then how you left your story *is* your story, and you had better not forget it.

Now I want to speak of another poem that is a landmark both in the story I am dealing with and in my own consciousness of poetry and of the world. This is the poem called "Maple Syrup," written about twenty-five years after "Elegy for Wesley Wells." The poem tells about an experience shared by a couple designated merely as "we." Since I am observing no critical conventions here, I will say that this "we" refers to the poet Donald Hall and the poet Jane Kenyon, who have returned to the house of Donald Hall's grandparents Kate and Wesley Wells. The two poets, married to each other, will live their life together in this house on this farm, relinquished and immortalized in the "Elegy" so many years before. In the poem "Maple Syrup" they go through the house together, to "the back chamber" full of artifacts and relics, and then down into "the root cellar," where they find a quart of maple syrup left there by Wesley Wells. And here I must let the poem speak:

> Today
> we take my grandfather's last
> quart of syrup
> upstairs, holding it gingerly,
> and we wash off twenty-five years
> of dirt, and we pull
> and pry the lid up, cutting the stiff
> dried rubber gasket, and dip our fingers
> in, you and I both, and taste
> the sweetness, you for the first time,
> the sweetness preserved, of a dead man . . .

We (that is, now, the poet and his readers) have come a long way from "Elegy for Wesley Wells." We have left the immortality of art and have come, by way of a sort of mortalization, to a communion of lovers with one another and with the dead, which is to say that we have come to a marriage rite, joining two mortals to one another, to a place, and to other mortals, bringing them perhaps within imaginable reach of a more authentic idea of immortality. Donald Hall, who in the "Elegy" is maybe a sort of bard, has now become, in the full and mysterious sense, a love poet. Or we might say that, having started out to be a professional, he has become an amateur, working (like the best kind of professional) for love. The sign of this is that the memory of Wesley Wells, once elegized into a mental landscape of the finished past, has become a living faculty of the poet's mind and imagination. The sweetness of the dead man, now, is not preserved in an artifact but in the lives of those who taste it.

One more thing. Because this rite of marriage occurs in this story, it does not give new life just to the couple, who now enter into its "one flesh"; it gives new life also to the dead and to an old house. It matters that this is an old house that is familiar to the bridegroom. If the house had been sold to strangers, according to the common destiny of old houses in our day, Wesley Wells' quart of syrup, if found, would have been thrown away. It would have seemed fearfully old and fearfully anonymous. To Don, and to Jane, trusting Don, it was mortal and everlasting, old and new, and sweet.

Having set up (so to speak) these two landmarks, an elegy and a celebration of marriage, I am much more moved than I would be by either of the poems alone, for I know the story that joins them. The two poems are joined by this story because the story of

Donald Hall had become also (to the degree that separate stories do converge) the story of Jane Kenyon.

What had happened was that these two stories had converged in one of the stages of Donald Hall's exile, teaching at the University of Michigan, and their convergence had made him free to return to the family house in New Hampshire. The agent of this freedom was Jane Kenyon, who said, according to her husband, "Why are we thinking of *here*, when there is New Hampshire?"

Not long after Don and Jane were settled at Eagle Pond, Don wrote to me, telling what they had done, and I wrote back some advice: Don't take on too much farming too quickly. Don has pointed out that the advice was wasted, since he did not intend to take on any farming at all—leaving me with the consolation that, anyhow, if he had needed it, it would have been good advice.

I am not sure when I met Jane, except that it was a good while ago, when she and Don were still heating their house with a very handsome wood-burning stove. I was on a speaking and reading trip in New England, and was able to stop by just for a short visit and lunch at a local eating place. I remember a tour of the house, but not much that was said. I remember being impressed by Jane's self-possession and dignity and quietness. These qualities continued to impress me after I knew her better. She was a writer, but she appeared to be watching "the literary world" without anxiety or great excitement.

Now the requirement of honesty is going to embarrass me, for I have to confess that I didn't read anything by Jane for a long time after I met her. For one reason, I felt a certain complicated sympathy for her—a poet who had set up shop smack in the middle of another poet's subject. The other poet's claim to this subject was well established; the other poet was her husband. It was easy to wish that she might have been, say, a painter. Another reason was that I liked her, and if she was a bad poet I did not want to know.

And then Bert Hornback invited Don and Galway Kinnell and Seamus Heaney and me to give a reading at the University of Michigan in January of 1986. For this there was a reason and a real reason. The reason was the public reading on Friday night. The real reason was that Bert wanted his students to have a late breakfast and conversation with the visiting poets on Saturday. In this age of careerist "research professors," Bert is a real teacher who thinks nothing of the trouble it takes to capture poets alive to talk with his students.

The visitors gathered at Bert's house for supper before the reading. When I came into the kitchen as the mingling and the talking began, Jane was standing by the refrigerator, watching the situation develop with the composure that I mentioned before. For the sake of political correctness I have been trying to avoid saying that Jane was beautiful, but of course she was, and of course I could see that she was. When we greeted each other, she said, "Wendell, I can't give you a hug. I have a bad cold." Baffled utterly by this generosity, I remember thinking that I had nothing better to do than catch a bad cold.

I have to go ahead and confess also that I do not greatly love literary occasions. The reading on Friday night was as readings are. The occasion beginning at breakfast on Saturday, however, was a literary occasion that surpassed itself. It was a *friendly* occasion, one of the loveliest that I have known. What I so liked about it was that everybody was talking for pleasure. There was no contention. Nobody defended a "position." There was much laughter. The students were hesitant to take part, but after a while they too entered into the conversation, and we had that additional pleasure.

Finally, late in the day, somebody—I don't remember who; it wasn't me—said, "Jane, why don't you read us a poem?"

Jane, who had been sitting almost outside the room, saying little, perhaps nothing at all, during the conversation, fished up from somewhere a page that she had brought with her and spread it open to read. For me, this was the only uncomfortable moment of that day. I don't remember what I thought, but it would have been like me to have started trying to think of some ambiguous compliment to make in case I thought the poem was bad— something like "Well, Jane, you certainly do write poetry." And then that quiet woman read beautifully her poem "Twilight: After Haying":

> Yes, long shadows go out
> from the bales; and yes, the soul
> must part from the body:
> what else could it do?
>
> The men sprawl near the baler,
> reluctant to leave the field.
> They talk and smoke,
> and the tips of their cigarettes
> blaze like small roses
> in the night air. (It arrived
> and settled among them
> before they were aware.)
>
> The moon comes
> to count the bales,
> and the dispossessed—

*Whip-poor-will, Whip-poor-will*
—sings from the dusty stubble.

These things happen . . . the soul's bliss
and suffering are bound together
like the grasses . . . .

The last, sweet exhalations
of timothy and vetch
go out with the song of the bird;
the ravaged field
grows wet with dew.

I hope I have adequately prepared you to imagine my relief.
Now I must ask you to imagine something else. However many
poets there may be who know from experience the subject of this
poem by Jane Kenyon, I surely am one of them. I have lived count-
less times through that moment at the end of a day's work when its
difficulty and heat and weariness take on a kind of sublimity and
you know that you are alive both in the world and in something
greater, when it is time to go and yet you stay on, charmed. I had
never tried to write a poem about that moment, and on that day,
when I had heard Jane read her poem, I knew that I would not
need to write one; Jane had written better about it than I could.
Sometimes I feel competitive or jealous when I *suspect* that somebody has written better than I can about something I know. When
I am *certain* that somebody has done so, then I am relieved and I
feel happy. "Twilight: After Haying" made me happy that day in
1986, and it has made me happy every time I have read it since.

Wittgenstein said that "In art [and, I assume, in writing about
art] it is hard to say anything as good as: saying nothing." I believe

and honor that, and I keep it in mind. But also we obviously need to speak from time to time of the things that have moved us. We need to wonder, for instance, why we remember some things and forget others. I have remembered Jane's reading of her poem that day, I think, because it was impossible to mistake the revelation of the event: Here was a poet present in her work with an authority virtually absolute. I don't mean that she is in the poem personally, but that all her gifts are in it: her quietness, gentleness, compassion, elegance, and clarity, her awareness of mystery, her almost severe good sense. This poem, like just about every one of her poems, is unconditional; it is poetry without qualification. It has no irony, no cynicism, no self-conscious reference to literary history, no anxiety about its place in literary history, no glance at the reader, no anticipation of the critic, no sensationalism, no self-apology or self-indulgence. How many poets of our time have been so unarmed as to say, "The moon comes / to count the bales . . ."? As she herself said (in the next poem of *The Boat of Quiet Hours*):

> These lines are written
> by an animal, an angel,
> a stranger sitting in my chair;
> by someone who already knows
> how to live without trouble
> among books, and pots and pans . . . .

—which is to say that she was authentically a poet of inspiration.

And this, to return to the story, seems to have settled pretty quickly the artistic problem of a shared life and subject. My wife Tanya has pointed out to me, from her knowledge of her own story, that Jane Kenyon had become, in fact, an exile in the very place that her husband had once felt himself to be exiled from. For a while after coming to Eagle Pond, she seems to have remembered "Ruth amid the alien corn":

> I'm the one who worries
> if I fit in with the furniture
> and the landscape.

And:

>           Maybe
> I don't belong here.
> Nothing tells me that I don't.

But such lines as these testify to a radically different approach to the problem of exile. The modern American version of exile is a rootless and wandering life in foreign lands or (amounting to about the same thing) in American universities. Jane Kenyon, like Ruth of old, understood her exile as resettlement. Very few American exiles, and not many American settlers, have asked "if I fit in with . . . the landscape" or worried about belonging to a place. And already one is aware of her originality, as one continues always to be aware of it. I mean "originality" in what I take to be the best sense: not the enactment of a certain kind of literary intention or ambition, but the grace to submit to influence—the influence of places, passages of scripture, works of art; the influence of all her subjects—and the grace and patience to find within herself the means to respond. Her contribution to this story is hers distinctly.

When I read a disparagement of the book *Otherwise* in *The Hudson Review*, I was offended, but also puzzled. How could anybody able to read fail to see the quality of that book? But after a while, I believe, I figured it out. Jane Kenyon's work, in fact, makes an unnegotiable demand upon a reader. It doesn't demand great intellect or learning or even sympathy; it demands quiet. It demands that in this age of political, economic, educational, and recreational pandemonium, and a concomitant rattling in the literary world, one must somehow become quiet enough to listen. Her poems raise unequivocally the issue of the quality of the poet's ear.

A true poem, we know, forms itself within hearing. It must live in the ear before it can live in the mind or the heart. The ear tells the poet when and how to break the silence, and when enough has been said. If one has no ear, then one has no art and is no poet. There is no appeal from this. If one has no ear, it does not matter what or how one writes. Without an ear, the traditional forms will not produce Andrew Marvell, nor will "free verse" give us William Carlos Williams.

Jane Kenyon had a virtually faultless ear. She was an exquisite master of the art of poetry. Her voice always carries the tremor of feeling disciplined by art. This is what over and over again enabled her to take the risk of plainness, or of apparent plainness. Her ear controls rhythm and sound, and also tone. It is tone as much as anything that makes one able to say what is unusual or unexpected. It is because of her perfection of tone that Jane Kenyon is able to say, "The moon comes / to count the bales . . ."

It is her perfection of tone that makes her poems able to accommodate sudden declarations of spiritual knowledge or religious faith, and that gives to so many of her poems the quality of prayer. It rules in her poems and passages of humor. It is the enabling principle in the political stroke of the poem entitled "Fat," and of the affirmation always present in her poems of sorrow. I am suggesting what I suppose cannot be demonstrated: that there is a practical affinity between the life of her soul and the technique of her poems.

The poems assemble themselves with a seeming arbitrariness, which is perhaps a comment. The poet looks at her subjects and experiences as they come to her and sees that they are ordinary; they are the stuff of life in this world; they could have come to anybody, at any time, in any order. They are revelations of ordinary satisfactions, joys, sufferings, deliverances which, in being revealed, become somehow numinous and resonant—extraordinary. In seeing that the poems are revelations, you see that they are not arbitrary but inevitable; in the course of the poem, form has occurred.

Sometimes the poems are poems of suspense; everything waits for the final line, as in the poem called "Things":

> The hen flings a single pebble aside
> with her yellow, reptilian foot.
> Never in eternity the same sound—
> a small stone falling on a red leaf.
>
> The juncture of twig and branch,
> scarred with lichen, is a gate
> we might enter, singing.
>
> The mouse pulls batting
> from a hundred-year-old quilt.
> She chewed a hole in a blue star
> to get it, and now she thrives . . . .
> Now is her time to thrive.

Things: simply lasting, then
failing to last: water, a blue heron's
eye, and the light passing
between them: into light all things
must fall, glad at last to have fallen.

The poem gathers itself as quietly as a snowy night, and then by the end a kind of dawn has come and everything is shining. That seems to be about all there is to say. This poem confirms for me as well as any I have read what I think is the fundamental fact of poetry: If you can explain it, it is something else.

Nor am I able to say much more about this story that I have undertaken to talk about. It is, I think, a good and valuable story. Two poets entered into it together, consenting to its foretold cost, lived it out, met its occasions, and made, separately and together, a life and a body of work that, for some of us, the world is now unimaginable without. They tasted a sweetness stored up by others; they stored up a sweetness to be tasted by others. And what are we friends and beneficiaries to say? Well, finally, maybe no more than "Thank you."

# Some Interim Thoughts about Gary Snyder's
## *Mountains and Rivers Without End*

———————————————— ∾ ————————————————

## (1996)

*Mountains and Rivers Without End* is an ambitious poem, and it fulfills its ambition partly by going about its task with a kind of modesty. Gary Snyder knows well what his work is or must try to be, and from start to finish he is busy doing his work. At no place in these 152 pages does one feel the poet calling attention to his skill or watching to see if he is being admired.

The poem takes shape within the tradition of Zen Buddhism, which Mr. Snyder has long studied and practiced, and it is informed by his extensive reading of geology, astronomy, biology, history, and the literature of Oriental and American Indian cultures.

Many readers by now take for granted that Mr. Snyder's mind and art have an Oriental ancestry, and this poem originates authentically in meditation on Chinese scroll paintings of endless mountains and rivers and in Dogen's *Mountains and Waters Sutra*. However, one cannot read this poem without feeling also the presence of its Western ancestors. It owes much to *The Cantos* and *Paterson*, though it seems to me a far neater poem with a more workmanly sense of purpose. *The Bridge* is back there in the pedigree somewhere, somehow, though I don't think Mr. Snyder's poem has a smidgeon of Crane's sentimental patriotism or his symbolistical confusion. And though it may be an understatement to say that Gary Snyder and John Milton are not alike, *Mountains and Rivers Without End* recalls and converses with the passages on the emerging world in *Paradise Lost*, Book VII.

I am confident that this poem has faults, and that it is no more definitive than any other poem—Milton's, for example—has been or will be. But this may be its fundamental proposition. If it should even for a moment forget its own condition of impermanence and claim to be the last word, it would be involved in a self-contradiction that would amount virtually to self-cancellation: It would disappear.

*Mountains and Rivers Without End* is not an endless poem because it cannot be—it ends, in fact, with perfect propriety and grace—but it is a poem about an unending subject: the great making of which we are the products, to which we contribute (not always or necessarily in our best interest), and to which the poem itself belongs. It is a poem about the poiesis of topography, cultures, cities, stories, dances, poems; about orogenesis, erosion, sedimentation; about composition; about travel.

Travel, in fact and metaphor, is its formal principle. The mountains are walking, says Dogen; they are traveling on water. And we, says Mr. Snyder, are walking on the mountains that are walking; we are floating down the rivers:

> *Walking on walking*
> *under foot     earth turns*
>
> *Streams and mountains never stay the same.*

People who think that "poetry makes nothing happen" will have to reckon again in reading this poem. Gary Snyder has been under the influence of his thought and work on this poem for forty years, during which he has not only worked to make things happen himself, but has influenced others who have been working to make things happen. And not only that. His poem is suffused, imbued, steeped in happening, the unending event of this world. How, as an effect of that event, with which it is totally preoccupied, could the poem not be in turn a cause?

Everything is in motion, everything is under influence, is being moved by something else, or by much else. Everything is "traveling." The great scroll painting *Endless Streams and Mountains*, now in the Cleveland Museum of Art, is a painting full of travelers on trails and waterways; the painting itself has traveled from place to place, from owner to owner; Mr. Snyder traveled to Cleveland to see it; he has borne it in mind during his other travels. And everything that happens happens in its time and in all time, and is never finished.

In Milton's version, the world was made at the beginning, once and for all; after that, human history would be the thing to watch. In Mr. Snyder's version, we are living in a world that is still and always being made; human history is not being made "on" or "in" the world, but is involved by intricate patterns of influence and causation in the continuous making of the world. This is an extremely important difference—morally, practically, and prosodically.

I am not dismissing Milton, whose work is eminent in my thoughts, and who is as instructive, dissident, and disturbing to intellectual conventions in our day as he was in his own. Read his lines on nature spirits (*Paradise Lost*, IV, 677–688) or on "knowing in measure" (VIII, 111–130), and you will see what I mean. His account of the creation of the world is an astonishing realization; I can't imagine that it will ever cease to matter. But one of the interesting things about Milton is his entanglement in the modern, dominantly urban and political world. Past the great Judaic legend of the acts of creation, Milton took the world for granted, as modern urban people and modern politics have steadfastly continued to do. The difference between John Milton and Gary Snyder is not primarily that between Western and Eastern cultures, or that between Europe and America, but that between a man who took the world for granted and a man who does not.

Mr. Snyder is by no means ignorant of the modern urban and political world, as several sections of this book amply show. But one thing that most distinguishes him as a poet is the extent to which he has accepted the influence of his experience of actual landscapes and cities, mountains and rivers. Milton was preeminently a scholar, and in his most productive years as a poet, by necessity of his blindness, he was a sedentary scholar; his task as a poet was to summon his great learning into imagination—to see inwardly what no human had seen before. Mr. Snyder too is a scholar, but he has always been a scholar walking and looking, telling us at times of things beyond sight, but telling us too what we will see in our everyday world if we will have the kindness to look. His poem is full of what is sometimes called "information," but it is information that has become real knowledge, knowledge worn in by experience. Much of what he has read about he has also seen, walked across, floated over. Several of the landscapes he has lived in he has also worked in.

*Mountains and Rivers Without End* is a poem keenly and amusedly conscious of participating in its subject. Its subject is ever-changing. By being about its subject, the poem assumes a certain power or responsibility to change it—perhaps for the better.

The poem thus refuses to be measured exclusively by literary or critical or scholarly standards. It freely and good-humoredly offers itself also to the measures of nature and experience. The statement implied by its publication is not an assertion but a question: not "This is the way it is" or "This is the way it seems to me" but "Is it not something like this? Does it not seem so to you?"

This poem is instructive. Whether or not it is "didactic" probably does not matter. It certainly is not didactic in the bad sense; it does not grab at your lapels or rant or condescend. What it teaches and indeed insists upon is the fluency of the world and therefore the pervasiveness of human influence and the moral problem of that influence. The world is always being changed, partly by us. We are always being changed by the world—and by the world as we have changed it. We cannot escape these forceful patterns of influence. The world cannot escape our influence or our effluents, including our poetry.

Since we are members of the natural world, what we do is "natural"—as cynics and technological determinists like to say. A beer can is as natural as a leaf, an atomic explosion as natural as a volcanic eruption, etc. Mr. Snyder concedes the point:

> trucks on the freeways,
> Kenworth, Peterbilt, Mack,
> rumble diesel depths,
> like boulders bumping in an outwash glacial river

But he points out, further, that these natural doings of ours can be dangerous to ourselves, not to mention the natural neighborhoods in which we must live. It is possible for humans to fabricate a human condition that obscures their natural condition:

> us and our stuff just covering the ground

so that we can know neither the mountains nor the Mountain Spirit. The solution to the moral problem (which is always more than moral) is to "become born-again natives" of the places where we live.

Mr. Snyder's poem will be disturbing also to people who think of the English sentence as an ultimate or adequate model of reality. What we have here, instead, is a syntax of verbal strokes, gesturing toward a reality that is not linear and directly causative like a conventional sentence, but instead is multidimensional and accumulative, is influential in all directions, like a geological formation, an ecosystem, a city, a culture. The difference is like that between the structure of a factory or a modern school and that of a family or a forest.

A fairly continuous and reassuring thread of merriment runs through this book, and part of it is the almost thematic upsetting of syntactic expectations. Fragments of syntax that at first seem to promise to become sentences lead into lists of items tumbling down the page. This is exactly as if what appears at a glance to be a stable slope is revealed, to a longer look, as a landslide—which is what every slope is, to a look that is long enough.

Mr. Snyder, of course, can write good sentences, and he has the confidence of this ability. His poem does not reject the artifice of syntactical "completeness" and closure—it is itself an artifice and must end—but puts it off, finds ways of procrastinating: lists, sentence fragments, sentences only begun, sentences caught up and carried on in structures that are not sentences. The book ends—humorously and gracefully acceding to its own provisional need to stop—with two plain, perfect sentences:

The space goes on.
But the wet black brush

> tip drawn to a point,
> > lifts away.

Mr. Snyder does not believe—as Teilhard de Chardin and many others have believed—that humans can "seize the tiller of the planet." *Mountains and Rivers Without End* is about the impossibility of such control—which, in a sense, it may demonstrate by its fragmentary syntax, its lists, its abrupt shifts of thought. And yet the poem does not imitate control-lessness. The poet's intelligence, skill, and artistic judgment are evident throughout, and from the earliest sections to the latest, his abilities increase. I leave the book, every time, with the sense that it is rhythmically and even musically coherent from start to finish. That is hard to demonstrate, obviously, but one of the signs of such coherence is economy, which is unarguably here. A wonderful amount is accomplished in these 152 pages; nothing is wasted. Another sign may be the frequent occurrence of passages that are eminently lyrical or memorable. I hesitate to quote because I will necessarily be quoting "out of context," but consider this prosodic astuteness of these lines:

> boat of the sun,
> the abt-fish, the yut fish,
> > play in the waves before it . . .

And the section entitled "afloat" opens with a lyric that spirals down, turning on rhymes and assonances:

Floating in a tiny boat
lightly on the water, rock with every ripple,

another skin that slides along the water
hung by sea and sky

green mountains turn to clouds
and slip slow by

two-mile saltwater channel
sucks and coils with the tide . . .

Thus it flows.

# In Memory: James Baker Hall

~

## (2009)

Jim Hall was, and so he will always be, my first literary friend. I began to know him in the fall of 1954, when he was a sophomore and I a junior at the University of Kentucky. And so we were friends for going on fifty-five years, by the measure of human life a long time. As I remember, our friendship began as follows. This, anyhow, is my earliest clear memory of Jim.

The two of us were in a writing class taught by Hollis Summers —"Dr. Summers," as we called him, and he called us "Mr. Hall" and "Mr. Berry." I sat somewhere near the front. Jim sat several rows back. He was blond-haired, deeply tanned, and athletic. His obvious fitness and strength, together with his striped T-shirts, somehow made him look bigger than he was. Until the event I am remembering, he hadn't said much, but sat with his arms folded, his lips pursed, intently looking. I knew him so far, only by sight, as "Mr. Hall."

For that class I wrote a story, "The Brothers," that told how Tom and Nathan Coulter blew up another boy's pet crow by inserting a dynamite cap with a piece of fuse into the crow's bunghole, as the story put it, lighting the fuse, and launching the crow into the air.

Maybe I had sense enough to know what a piece of mischief

that story would be in that situation, but I doubt it. I believe I merely thought, with a sort of roughneck innocence, that the story was funny. But when Dr. Summers had finished reading the story to the class, and a voice stridently humane had begun to retaliate from the front row, the formerly quiet Mr. Hall leapt out of his seat, emitting laughter and other subverbal noises, and crying, "No, no, no, no!" He made other shouts to the effect that the story was just right, should be let alone, should not be tampered with, etc. It was some time before Dr. Summers could subdue the class to the level of critical discourse.

Even subtracting the humane objection, nothing I have written in the fifty-five years since has been received so enthusiastically. Of course my story and Jim's response were boys' work, but that day began our life's work of being friends. From then until Jim left for Stanford in the fall of 1957, we carried on an endless, eager, strenuous conversation about everything that interested us, but we talked mostly about writing and writers.

In the years that followed that conversation went on and on, sometimes face to face, sometimes by mail, sometimes by telephone, through a good many meanders and a good many ups and downs. In a letter to me last December, Jim said, "We've been around a few barns in our journey together, huh! Sometimes going in the same direction, sometimes not. Sometimes in tandem, sometimes not."

That was Jim's last letter to me, and I believe it was so understood and so meant. In it you hear, not only his manner of speech, but his characteristic, passionate refusal to gloss over or leave out matters of difference. We certainly did have a journey together, and we certainly were not always going in tandem or in the same direction. But his candor about that gives a palpable verification to the letter's final words: "With love, in friendship."

When I try to reckon up my debt to Jim, as if to itemize the account and end with a sum, I always have to settle for "immeasurable." Our conversation, starting so early and lasting so long, I count as an immense gift in itself. But it also made Jim one of the people I have most frequently talked to in my thoughts. His presence in my mind has been one of the tests of whatever I have thought. And I have always read his writing and studied his photographs, looking through the work for the man, wondering, as his artistry grew, how it had grown, how he had come to know what he knew, how he had learned to do what he did.

As I seem to be confessing, I have grown or aged into difficulty in distinguishing between art and life. The reason may be that the difference is not always as neat or as convincing as I used to think. When we make our art we are also making our lives, and I am sure that the reverse is equally true. When Jim wrote in one of his more recent poems that "Light and dark became my sudden work," so brilliantly using that adjective, he was talking about photography surely, but for me the line has a larger resonance. I hear it referring also to his long and arduous work of making his life by drawing it from darkness into light, and so making it whole.

Knowing Jim, among other things, has made me extremely doubtful of that word "understanding." I don't want to say the last word about anything—including, especially, Jim. But I believe, and on good evidence, that Jim's work of life-making succeeded. It was a wondrous accomplishment. During his last months, his illness obviously made him dependent, first and most upon Mary Ann, and also upon doctors and medicines, but within himself, in what he was calling his "inner life," he was freestanding and whole, gracious and graceful.

He knew clearly how ill he was, but he did not make a fiction or an etiquette of ignoring his illness. It was as it was, and he acknowledged it freely. But in my several visits to the house on Dividing Ridge and in our more than several conversations on the phone, I never caught the faintest hint of self-sorrow. We talked, as we always had, of things of interest. He had what he needed: Mary Ann and their life together in their good place. He was living every day with all the life he had, and not asking for more. He had gone beyond admirable. He was exemplary.

And so, with love, in friendship, thank you, Jim. And, Mary Ann, thank you.

# Against the Nihil of the Age

~

## (2001)

*Against the* nihil
*One candle-flame, one blade of grass,*
*One thought suffices*
*To affirm all.*

Kathleen Raine has been so lucid and indispensable a commentator on the work of Blake, Yeats, and other poets, and so devoted a defender and teacher of their tradition, that a reader of her own poetry may be led astray by preconceptions. I have to admit, anyhow, that my early reading of her poems was made awkward by my supposition that I would find her to be more like, or more akin to, Blake or Yeats than in fact she is.

This sort of confusion is embarrassing whenever it occurs, because it is correctable by recognition of an obvious truth: Being a poet oneself is nothing like studying the work of other poets, closely allied with them as one may be. However learned one may become in the lineages of thought or faith or art that sustain one's life and work, one must approach every new work of one's own as a sort of innocent, trying to see what truth, old and long-honored though it is, might be found shining anew in the places, events, companions, and memories of one's own life.

*The Collected Poems of Kathleen Raine* (published in England by Golgonooza Press and in the United States by Counterpoint), more than most books, is the record of the struggle of its own making. It has been a complicated and a momentous struggle, and to say what it has involved and accomplished may at the same time provide an accurate enough evaluation of the book.

From early in her life Kathleen Raine's vocation pretty clearly was to become a poet of religious vision—or, more precisely, a poet of Imagination in the high sense in which Blake used that term: the "Divine Humanity," the "Poetic Genius," the "Spirit of Prophecy," the power of inspiration, the vision of eternal things, our means of conversing with Paradise. The power of Imagination is to see things in their eternal aspect; it is to know the timeless as it "moves through time," the eternal presence that is both in and outside time and that comprehends the things we know and remember. All ways of expressing this power and this presence probably are incomplete, and yet they suggest to us a completeness that the arts of imagination have always striven toward: "That human mystery all arts praise." The poet of Imagination in this sense is divested, almost by definition, of several concerns that have adhered to the contemporary "profession" of poetry: art for art's sake, fashions and schools, technical innovation and intellectual display and "originality" as valuable in themselves. This poet seems to have relinquished all of those without regret or a backward look. Her technical virtues are economy, plain eloquence, an unostentatious command of the prosodic and musical means of her art. This artistry she has put forthrightly into the service of her calling and her subjects.

The predicament of a visionary poet at any time is difficult. The poems one desires to write cannot be written merely by desire, or by intellect or learning or will or technical artistry—though they also cannot be written *without* desire, intellect, learning, will, and artistry. Beyond all these, inspiration must come, and when it comes one must be ready. The readiness is everything. It involves everything listed above, plus a life's work.

To be a visionary poet in the industrial age, in what Kathleen Raine has called "this post-real world," is a predicament of greater difficulty than before. It is to be consigned, as a poet, to a way of images in a time of the desecration of all images, a time when "the sacred lineaments grow faint, the outlines crumble / and the golden heavens grow dim . . ."

The most fundamental of these desecrations has been the reduction of the human image, which we once understood as the image of God, to an image merely of humanity itself as a "higher animal"—with the implied permission to be more bewildered, violent, self-deluded, destructive, and self-destructive than any of the animals. From the desecration of that image, the desecration of the world and all its places and creatures inexorably follows. For it appears that, having once repudiated our primordial likening to the maker and preserver of the world, we don't become merely higher animals, merely neutral components of the creation-by-chance of the materialists, but are ruled instead by an antithetical likeness to whatever unmakes and fragments the world.

In this situation a poet, as a maker or perceiver of images, is by definition not capable of the modern indifference to the world of images and its fate, an indifference which may wear either of two faces: that of a facile and disengaged "spirituality," which is essentially unimagining, or that of the now-dominant scientific and industrial materialism, which destroys the material world by breaking all images into ever smaller and more abstract parts.

Nor can she have very easily or very soon the solace of a perfect resolution of personal struggle within faith, within art, that was still possible, and that seems to have ended, in the seventeenth century, when the wandering or rebellious soul, as if by second nature, could find its way to rest in God:

> But as I raved and grew more fierce and wild
>> At every word,
> Methought I heard one calling, *Child*!
>> And I replied, *My Lord*.

Or:

> They also serve who only stand and wait.

We have continued to have poets of faith and vision, but in a time of the desecration of images, resolution has come as the result of a more and more arduous and costly struggle, of shoring up fragments against our ruin.

This is a time also, as Wordsworth said in his preface to the second edition of *Lyrical Ballads*, of "the increasing accumulation of men in cities, where the uniformity of their occupations produces a craving for extraordinary incident," a "degrading thirst after outrageous stimulation." Our time's widespread but little-acknowledged conviction that importance and even significance increase with violence discourages and obscures the paramount truths of human experience, which come only quietly into a quieted mind.

At the time when Kathleen Raine—then studying botany, physiology, and chemistry at Cambridge—was first publishing her poems, the most prominent poets of her generation had accepted scientific rationalism, materialism, and reductionism as describing the outer boundary of legitimate human experience. The idea that life is coextensive with its physical forms, and that these forms are or will be completely intelligible within the terms of reductionist science, had already become an intellectual and academic orthodoxy. This orthodoxy still prevails in the universities and in the enterprise of science, technology, and marketing which constitutes industrial culture. Its insignia is the refusal to take seriously anything that was taken seriously in the past. It is most famously represented in poetry, I suppose, by the cocky braininess and condescension of Auden's elegy for Yeats. The result, of which the evidence is now inescapable, is a world in which work based on the recognition of sanctity is less and less possible—which is to say, a world in which we are less and less able to keep from destroying even things of economic or scientific value.

For a time, during her Cambridge years, Kathleen Raine was drawn to this orthodoxy and tried to accommodate herself to it, writing, she has said, "complex, tight, unfeeling, objective little poems." But eventually she rebelled and began the effort of "half a lifetime" to free herself. Why did she do this?

She did it, evidently, because by the time she went to Cambridge her life had already been rich in experience and influence. It was her own past finally that instructed her to face away from the dispirited intellectuality that she had encountered at Cambridge. Both of her parents had loved poetry. Shakespeare, Milton, and the romantic poets had been honored, read, and quoted in her childhood home, and her Scottish mother knew the border ballads. In her childhood also she had spent some time in a rural part of Northumbria where she felt at home, and where she came to know with a child's intimacy the nature and culture of a traditional landscape, soon to come under domination by the alien economy of the rapidly industrializing world. In *Farewell Happy Fields*, the first of her autobiographical volumes, she remembers this change: "The Essex Maidens, the white foam of cow parsley, the muddy lanes bordering misty ploughed fields, farms with walnut trees, chestnut avenues, all that old slowly traced, slowly matured human pattern of life lived from generation to generation," was replaced by a "new pattern [that] no longer bore any relationship to shelter of hill or fall of stream . . ." She had seen the old pattern being destroyed, but she nevertheless had seen it. She never forgot it.

And so when she encountered the scientific materialism of Cambridge, she encountered it as a young woman with a cultural past that she had experienced fully and had received as an influence, though she was not yet aware of its importance. Her later recognition of its importance probably informs her "Letter to Pierre Emmanuel," in which she says, "To be a barbarian is to have no past." In a recent conversation with Grevel Lindop, she said that, at Cambridge, "I didn't distinguish between my love of flowers[,] from the point of view of poetry and beauty[,] and studying botany . . ." She thus was able to escape the academic orthodoxy because she was never entirely in it. A friend of mine has called my attention to a sentence from George Orwell's letter "What Is Science?" which suggests that neither Kathleen Raine's dissidence nor the reasons for it were unique. Speaking of some unnamed British and American physicists who refused to work on the atom bomb project, Orwell wrote: "I think it would be a safe guess that all of them were people with some kind of general cultural background, some acquaintance with history or literature or the arts—in short, people whose interests were not, in the current sense of the word, purely scientific."

She freed herself of the influence of materialism by remaining under the influence of her past, but also by cultivating more and more consciously the poetic kinships that would support her own work. One can trace in this volume numerous influences that have affected directly not only her thoughts and perceptions, but also at various stages her ways of shaping her poems: Old English spells and riddles, the ballads, Milton, the romantic poets, Hopkins; she owes a particular, if limited, debt to Wordsworth's immortality ode; and of course her most acknowledged affinities have been with Blake and Yeats.

But as I began by saying, knowledge of her long attention and service to the work of Blake and Yeats can cause a reader to come to her work with wrong expectations. Her study of their work has unquestionably helped her to form her own, and her debt to them (like theirs to her) is great. Her own poems certainly belong to their tradition, and carry it forward. But her work is also different from theirs. To make that difference has been crucial to the development of her poetry, and to see it is indispensable to a reader.

On page six of the first volume of *Blake and Tradition*, she writes: "Blake saw nature through symbol, not symbol through nature." The opposite, I think, is true of her. Because of her persistent remembrance of the landscapes of her childhood and her intimate knowledge of natural history, her clear perception of the natural world wherever she has encountered it and her affection for it, she has seen symbols (when she has seen them) through or in nature. For example, water in these poems nearly always has the power of a symbol, and yet it always has also the local character of a particular seashore or stream. I don't think her poems emerge so directly from *systems* of symbols or beliefs as she has shown those of Blake and Yeats to have done. More than either of them, because of her disposition and circumstances, she is a poet of the world of experience. Her allegiance to the traditional wisdom that informs their work is no less than theirs, but the underlying drama of her work is shaped less by a system of ideas or symbols than by archetypal stories: primarily by that of Demeter and Persephone, but also by the stories of Eve and of Psyche and Cupid—stories of loss and restoration.

Her fidelity to her own experience and her own way of perceiving is one of the major qualities of her poetry. As a poet of experience, she is without recourse either to the purity of the mystics or to the abstract coherences of the philosophers and theologians. She may believe, as Plato did, that the things of this world are only shadows of their eternal archetypes, but still she loves many of the things of this world. The True, the Good, and the Beautiful exist immortally in their archetypal forms—she never doubts this—but they also manifest themselves in the creatures and works of this world, and she loves these manifestations and is ever grateful for them. She grieves over their loss, and rejoices at their recovery. Demeter, as Milton said, must seek the lost Persephone "through the world," not in thought or vision only.

This poet can speak confidently enough of "unsolid matter," but she also confronts without flinching the fundamental ambiguities of experience: the dream-likeness of the world, the world-likeness of our dreams, the dream-likeness and world-likeness of our memories. She is ever aware of the possibilities of illusion and error. She is affectionate and sorrowful and delighted. She confronts her limits and failures with remorse but also with humor, and the overturning of expectations, even her own, with pleasure. Not one of the book's highest moments, but one of its best, is this couplet:

Incredible that anything exists—this hotch-potch
World of marvels and trivia, and which is which?

With the same candor, but with something like despair, she
recorded in 1951 her failure to see, like Blake, "a world in a grain of
sand":

> I have come seeking
> The infinite cipher
> And sum of all wisdom
> Inscribed on a grain
> Of sand . . .

But she is walking, according to the poem's title, "On a Shell-strewn
Beach," where she finds that she lacks the necessary vision:

> I have found
> A myriad particles
> And each is all
> That can ever be told,
> But all are inscribed
> With a signature
> That I cannot read . . .

This, however, is the experience of a day. At other times she is more
favored, and the desired insight comes, as in these lines from "In
My Seventieth Year":

> Light falling on a London wall
> Filtered through curtains or through leaves
> Stirred in the gently moving air,

Or circles spreading in a pool
About each falling drop of rain,
A sparrow basking in the sun—
Each is the presence of the all,
And all things bear the signature
Of one unfathomable thought
Lucid as universal light . . .

The presence of both of these poems in this book gives us, I think, a way to understand the character of the "I" who is speaking in the poems and the quality of the voice. The "I" can sometimes be very general; sometimes it can be so inclusive as to remind at least this American reader of the "I" of Whitman's "Song of Myself." But though the "I" at its most personal never indulges in the "confessional" self-exposure of much recent verse, it is also never entirely impersonal. It seems always quietly to be insisting on the personal basis of the writer's experience. Her voice is not as rhetorical as the voices of Blake and Yeats; she is, I think, too sternly honest, particularly about herself, to adopt the self-assurance of a highly rhetorical form of speech; she speaks sometimes from the upper reaches of perception and inspiration, but even then, and especially if one is keeping in mind the whole book as the context of the individual poems, one hears her speaking as herself, a mortal and fallible woman, grateful for the light and clarity she has been given.

The insistently, persistently *human* quality of this voice makes it trustworthy. This voice might be affected by, but it could not produce, poems such as Yeats' "The Choice" or "Sailing to Byzantium," both of which deal with choices that, for actual people, don't exist. My purpose here is not to praise one poet at another's expense; I am merely trying to say something precise about the quality of the voice speaking in Kathleen Raine's poems. "The Choice" is a valuable poem, I suppose, but to me it is valuable mostly as an example of a fictitious choice between "perfection of the life, or of the work," a choice that does damage to people who think they can actually make it. On the other hand, I love and greatly admire "Sailing to Byzantium," and the older I get the more I love and admire it, even though I think it proposes another choice—between "dying generations" and "monuments of unageing intellect"—that exists only in sonority. My point is that the tension of the drama underlying Kathleen Raine's poems comes precisely from the humble and humbling recognition that now, in time, in this world, no such choice exists. She has willingly received into her poetry her great reverence for the monuments of unageing intellect without ever repudiating her grief for the dying generations. This is her humanity and her honesty which establish the tone of her voice, and which—as I will try to show—set the terms of her triumph.

Perhaps because she did not distinguish between her love for nature and her study of it, she also took into her poetry something of her scientific education that would affect her thought and her work profoundly and would never be absent from it. This was her understanding of nature as process. The creatures of nature that she loves she sees both as they momentarily are and as embodiments of the long becoming, into which as they momentarily are they will disappear. As a poet, but from what she learned as a scientist, she knows

> with what infinite gentleness being flows
> Into the forms of nature, and unfolds
> Into the slowly ascending tree of life
> That opens, bud by bud, into the sky.

She is working here as a poet of incarnation at the most physical level. But this knowledge makes available to her a set of analogues that she never ceases to explore: The way being flows into its creaturely forms is analogous to the way the cultural and historical birthright enters into human minds and is passed on, and to the way souls enter the world, and to the way the Holy Spirit, Milton's "Heav'nly Muse," Blake's "Imagination," or what Kathleen Raine eventually will call "the Presence," passes by inspiration into human acts and works.

Her old love of the ballads, under the influence of this resonant sense of incarnation, gives us, twenty-five years later, "Maire Macrae's Song":

> The singer is old and has forgotten
> Her girlhood's grief for the young soldier
> Who sailed away across the ocean,
> Love's brief joy and lonely sorrow:
> The song is older than the singer.
>
> The song is older than the singer
> Shaped by the love and the long waiting
> Of women dead and long forgotten
> Who sang before remembered time
> To teach the unbroken heart its sorrow.

The girl who waits for her young soldier
Learns from the cadence of a song
How deep her love, how long the waiting.
Sorrow is older than the heart,
Already old when love is young:
The song is older than the sorrow.

This is perfect and beautiful, and no more needs to be said about it.

She seems always to have been capable of closely wrought, musical verse, as in this poem or, much earlier, "The World." But as both idea and subject, the incarnational principle seems, at least at first, to have required a looser, roomier kind of poem, affording her the scope necessary to accumulate details and demonstrate what she is talking about. In "Northumbrian Sequence," from which I have already quoted, the subject is not only the way being "flows / Into the forms of nature," but also the way being overflows its forms:

The sleeper at the rowan's foot
Dreams the darkness at the root,
Dreams the flow that ascends the vein
And fills with world the dreamer's brain.

. . . . . . . . . . . . . . . .

And the burden is so great
Of the dark flow from without,
Of sun streaming from the sky
And the dead rising from the root,
Of the earth's desire to be
In this dreaming world incarnate
That world has overflowed the trees.

. . . . . . . . . . . . . . . .

The sleeper of the rowan tree
As full of dream as tree can bear
Sends the bird singing in the air
As full of world as song can cry,
And yet the song is overflowed . . .

We tend to think that form in art should, and in nature does, perfectly contain its content. But what if, in reality, life in nature does
overflow its forms, and can continue only by so doing? And what
if the artist, in mere faithfulness and honesty, must struggle to
make this overflowing the subject of art? And is it not the most
fundamental knowledge of a poet of inspiration that inspiration
always exceeds the formal attempt to contain and express it? Such
questions disturb profoundly the processes both of thought-
making and verse-making.

What we are seeing in "Northumbrian Sequence" is another
significant and lasting result, maybe the most important result,
of Kathleen Raine's scientific education: her revolt, increasingly
conscious and principled as her work goes on, against any form
of reductionism. In "Exile," the third of "Three Poems on Illusion," this revolt is made explicit. She has begun by speaking of her
childhood knowledge of the creatures, when "They never wearied
of telling their being," and then, in exile from the clarity of that
innocent knowledge, she goes on to speak directly of her experience in the laboratory:

But still the mind, curious to pursue
Long followed them, as they withdrew
Deep within their inner distances,
Pulled the petals from flowers, the wings from flies,

Hunted the heart with a dissecting-knife
And scattered under a lens the dust of life;
But the remoter, stranger
Scales iridescent, cells, spindles, chromosomes,
Still merely are:
With hail, snow-crystals, mountains, stars,
Fox in the dusk, lightning, gnats in the evening air
They share the natural mystery,
Proclaim I AM, and remain nameless.

I think this is an astonishing passage, one of the high places of the history of poetry as I know it, and certainly of my own reading. It is a "breakthrough"—in the right direction—full of the resonance of the poet's relief and exhilaration at having found at hand the language for what has long needed saying. But, wonderful as it is, it does not have the fineness of finish or the assurance that the best of her later work will have. The marks of struggle are on it; the syntax is tentative in places, and there is a sense of the words piling up, as if she is asking of the poem or herself something not yet fully available to her.

It is not an insult to the art of poetry to recognize that sometimes a work that is technically imperfect can at the same time be indispensable. Such a recognition would be misleading or beside the point if the only proper concern of poetry were the production of technically perfect poems. But the proper concern of poetry is also to purify and vivify and renew the language, to enlarge the possibility of consciousness by enlarging the capability of speech. This poem, though technically imperfect, is nevertheless of vital importance because it revives the language needed to speak of the inherent sanctity of created things.

Kathleen Raine is one of the poets whose work contradicts the idea (too often repeated) that a poet exists to write one or two or a handful of "great" or anthologizable poems. Unless we don't mind overlooking most of the value and excitement of it, we mustn't think of her *Collected Poems* as a heap of ore from which critics will eventually smelt enough gold for a ring or two. Who can know? Maybe eventually they will. But for us, now, the work of chief importance is the whole book, which is a landmark. The book records the effort of a long lifetime to learn to see and speak in a way the poet could not see and speak when she began—in a way, I think, that no poet of her time could see and speak when she began.

When I spoke of her "breakthrough" in the poem "Exile," I meant that she had broken the narrow boundaries of materialist and empirical thought, and had come into the real presence of the creatures of the natural world. She had done this by recognizing in each of them the immanence of that originating and sustaining Presence that in her later work will be so named. She had seen that every creature participates in, represents, and speaks for the I AM of creation who spoke to Moses from the burning bush. She had begun the rectification of her vision of nature. Now she began to see the world in the dimension of the "everlasting to everlasting" that is present in every creature at every moment.

There are several ways by which one might follow her development from such crucial poems as "Northumbrian Sequence" and "Exile," published in *The Year One* in 1952, to the new poems at the end of *The Colleceted Poems*, published in 2000, for this book has something of the character of a "braided stream" of several channels and islands. To try to write about it in an essay of reasonable length is to realize how much one *might* say about it that one is not going to be able to say. But probably the most useful thread to pick up is the theme of Paradise, which gives the book its underlying mythic and dramatic structure.

The biographical starting point of this theme is the poet's childhood stay in Northumbria. She recalls this experience again and again and always thinks of it as paradisal. In *The Land Unknown*, the second volume of her autobiography, she suggests how this memory becomes for her a story: "Those who in childhood have known the state of Paradise perhaps always expect to find again what was once so simply there." And in *Farewell Happy Fields*, she speaks of Paradise as "a state of being in which outer and inner reality are at one, the world in harmony with imagination." Where she parts company with Wordsworth, of course, is not in the state but in the story, in her expectation of finding again, in exile, what was lost.

The cultural descendants of the Bible can't speak of Paradise without remembering the first couple's expulsion from Eden, and Kathleen Raine is ever mindful of that story, in the Bible and in Milton, of "The locked gate and the flaming sword . . ." But in her mind Paradise is also indelibly associated with Demeter and her seeking "through the world." And so the resolution here is not specifically Christian, not dependent on the restoration by the "one greater Man" of Milton's poem. But some of the poems in this book also work a variation on the Demeter myth, for the Persephone sought by the poet is what she sees as her truest self, herself as a child:

> It is myself
> I leave behind,
> My mother's child,

Simple, unlearned,
Whose soul's country
Was these bright hills,
This northern sky.

And so the story underlying the poems of this book is that of
a woman exiled from Paradise, wandering through the world in
search of the innocent, undivided, profoundly illuminated world,
or world of vision, that she has known and cannot forget. To
remember is her actuating principle. It is also her anguish. The
poems in this book never turn away from the world of exile and
grief—which for her, as for Blake, Hopkins, and others, is now
unavoidably the machine-world of our own time, but which for
her is also the world of "Dear human faces that must die." Her
grief is enforced by the memories of the lost clear world of her
childhood, of lost love, and by the thought of what might have
been. Without the paradisal memory there would be no grief; but
it is grief that preserves and clarifies the memory of her joy, and
gives it life and value.

As these themes of loss and memory and grief work themselves out through the years and the pages, the poet learns to see
in memory itself, however painful, a recovery of what has been
lost, as she learns to see also the eternal Presence manifested in
the things of time. That Presence and its Paradise are always present to Imagination, though not always to human imaginers. And
as the book never turns away from the world of exile and grief, it
also never turns away from the possibility of moments of vision
when Paradise is again present and visible to the imaginer, and she
knows that

All stands in two worlds, and the ground
Of Paradise is everywhere.

The truest wisdom comes, one might say, when Demeter, without ceasing to be herself or forgetting her experience, sees with the vision of Persephone; *because* she grieves, because she does not forget or give up her search, she is permitted to see what is paradisal even in the world as it is:

Not lonely, now that I am old,
But still companioned like a child
Whose morning sun was friend enough,
And beauty of a field of flowers
Expressive as my mother's face.

In such moments of vision "then" is "here and now," eternity comes alight in time, and in every creature is the seed of all: "one apple-bud / Opens the flower of the world . . ."

In contemplating the theme of Imagination or paradisal vision as it is carried throughout *The Collected Poems*, one is impressed by the extent to which the literary quality of the work is affected by concerns that far surpass the present interests of the "literary world." These poems, like George Herbert's, could be shelved as justly with religious writings as with poetry. But they might with equal justice be read by people interested in the politics of conservation or the methodologies of land use. Lines such as the following are certainly poetry, but it is hard to keep them confined in that category for they are full of implications that are religious, economic, and (as we may hope) scientific:

As you leave Eden behind you, remember your home,
For as you remember back into your own being
You will not be alone; the first to greet you
Will be those children playing by the burn,
The otters will swim up to you in the bay,
The wild deer on the moor will run beside you.
Recollect more deeply and the birds will come,
Fish rise to meet you in their silver shoals . . .

I am trying to say what I think has been accomplished by the life's work that this book represents, and singling out the theme of Paradise has helped me to do that. But I am afraid that in doing so I have made the book's achievement seem too deliberate and too neat. I would not like to obscure either the difficulty and length of the poet's effort or its variousness. There are several other strands that one could follow through this book, and all are finally indispensable to its development and significance. One that is most important is the compounding of the poet's sense of herself as a woman writing, culminating in these lines at the end of "Testimony":

> This woman whose hand writes words not mine,
> bequeathed by multitude of the once living
> who knew, loved, understood, and told
> Meanings passed down
> To the yet to come, whose faces I shall not see,
> Yet whom as I write these words I already am.

Another vital strand, always related to the theme of paradisal vision, is the development of what I earlier called her revolt against reductionism, or her long unlearning of that way of thought. She begins this consciously, in poems from *The Year One*, written about fifty years ago, by dispensing with the specifically scientific impediments to recognizing the presence of the creatures. One cannot, of course, come into the presence of anything by dissection or analysis or the cataloging of parts or the assaying of predictability. But she goes further. As she grows older, and grows in knowledge and in practice, the paradisal vision ceases to be a memory and ideal that she seeks for; it becomes instead a blessing that she accepts as a native property of her life and mind, but accepts always with the understanding that it comes only unexpectedly, in its own time:

> I had meant to write a different poem,
> But, pausing for a moment in my unweeded garden,
> Noticed, all at once, paradise descending in the morning
>     sun,
> Filtered through leaves,
> Enlightening the meagre London ground, touching with
>     green
> Transparency the cells of life.
> The blackbird hopped down, robin and sparrow came,
> And the thrush . . .

Later (apparently) comes the poem "Garden Simurgh," in which the poet puts out nuts for the blue-tits, but only the sparrows come, and she is disappointed. But then she finds in herself a sufficient tenderness even for

> these two-a-farthing sparrows
> Each feather wearing the carelessly-worn signature

Of the universe that has brought them here to the
    Lord's table
With such delight, never doubting their welcome . . .

The world overturns our expectations simply because the world
is large and our expectations necessarily are small. This the world
teaches us every day. But the world does not teach us to welcome
so humbling a truth. The triumph of this book is that it has taught
its poet to welcome these overturnings of expectation, and the
reason for this also is plain and lowly, though perhaps always long
to learn: You can't see "paradise descending in the morning sun"
by expecting to do so.

The poet follows the logic of this realization to its limit. As she
rejects the reductionism of scientific materialism and of her own
expectations, so finally she rejects as reductionistic all systems of
thought and belief:

But all we know is hearsay, save
The record in the Book of Life:
Where Sandaig burn runs to the shore,
Where tern and eider rest secure
On their far island salt and bare . . .

And:

No written page more true
Than blade of grass and drop of dew.

And:

I believe nothing—what need
Surrounded as I am with marvels of what is,
This familiar room, books, shabby carpet on the floor,

Autumn yellow jasmine, crysanthemums, my mother's
    flower,
Earth-scent of memories, daily miracles,
Yet media-people ask, 'Is there a God?'

As she more and more directly confronts the marvelous, rejecting
the inevitably reductive forms of human comprehension, and as
her sense of the greatness of the mystery of being increases, a tenderness of charity grows in her and reaches out unaskingly to the
creatures: flowers always, her cat, the sparrows who come to the
feed she had prepared for the blue-tits.

The last poem in the book, and the most recent, is the "Millen-
nial Hymn to the Lord Shiva," which anathematizes the world as
we have made it, but in doing so affirms all that she has stood for
and spoken for. It is a plea for the overturning of all our reductive
expectations, an invocation of the cleansing fire that is both end
and beginning:

Our elected parliaments
Parrot their rhetoric
Of peace and democracy
While the truth we deny
Returns in our dreams
Of Armageddon,
The death-wish, the arms-trade,
Hatred and slaughter
Profitable employment
Of our thriving cities,

The arms-race
To the end of the world
Of our postmodern, post-Christian,
Post-human nations,
Progress to the nihil
Of our spent civilization.

. . . . . . . . . . . . .

To whom shall we pray
When our vision has faded
But the world-destroyer,
The liberator, the purifier?

There is a triumph in the ability to see these dissolutions as a necessary cleansing, and this is arguably the climactic poem of the book, leaving little more to be said; but, perhaps for those reasons, it is not a representative poem. I would like to end my essay with something representative; and since I have been quoting mostly fragments, which was necessary but unfair, I want to quote a whole poem:

## Woodruff

Today the Presence
Has set before me
Woodruff's white foam
Of petals immaculate,
Fourfold stars numberless
Open life's centres,
In a London garden
They grow in a spring wood
Before the city and after

Machines whose noise
Tears the sky.
The white stars
Do not hear; they tell me
'The woods are always.'
Lily of the valley
Feels for loam of leaves
And the blackbirds
Build anew, repair
The rents we tear
In times and places.
Immemorial woods
Are here, are near,
The white stars cross
The invisible frontier:
'Come to us,' the flowers say,
'We will show you the way.'

This is a beautifully realized poem. It runs a certain risk in its plainness, its closeness to prose, but there is not a dead or an inert line in it. It is utterly without technical ostentation, but its assonances and rhymes sound and resound and have their influence. It is a nature poem about the unnatural modern urban world. In speaking of the four-petaled flowers as "fourfold stars," the poet commemorates Blake's concept of the Imagination: "fourfold in . . . supreme delight." The flowers of the woodruff are accepted as instructors, like the "lilies of the field" in Matthew 6:28, that come effortlessly into glory. They speak for the forest, the original world, of which London, however old it is, however old it may become, is a temporary interruption. The blossoms and the birds manifest the ongoing presence of the life of nature, which manifests the

Presence of the Spirit that informs all things, including the mind of Kathleen Raine and this poem, in the few short lines of which she seems to have compacted all she has learned. And with what quietude of mastery she has done it!

# The Uses of Adversity

———————— ～ ————————

## (2006)

### *I.*

It has been useful to me to think of *As You Like It* and *King Lear* as versions of the same archetypal story, belonging to human experience both before and after the plays. This is the story: In the instituted life of a society "things fall apart" because the people of power have grown selfish, cruel, and dishonest. The effect of this is centrifugal; the powerless and the disempowered are sent flying from their settled domestic life into the wilderness or the world's wildness—the state of nature. Thus deprived of civil society and exposed to the harshness of the natural world and its weather, they suffer correction, and their suffering eventually leads to a restoration of civility and order.

The outline of this story is clearly apparent in *As You Like It*. In *King Lear* the story is subjected to nearly intolerable stresses, and yet the outline remains unbroken; it is the major source of the play's coherence and meaning. What I believe is the proper understanding of both plays depends on our ability to take seriously the assumptions of the archetypal story—on how we answer the following questions: Do all human societies have in them the seeds of their failure? Are those seeds likely to be the selfishness and dishonesty of the dominant people? Does failure typically reduce the society, or persons in it, to some version of the state of nature? And is there something possibly instructive and restorative in this reduction?

For most readers nowadays these questions will be an unwelcome dose. We have read some history, and we do not doubt that other societies have failed, but we are not much inclined to credit the possible failure of our own, even though we are less and less able to deny the implications of our propensity to waste or to mechanical violence, or of our entire dependence on cheap petroleum. We have pretty much made a virtue of selfishness as the mainstay of our economy, and we have provided an abundance of good excuses to dishonesty. Most of us give no thought to the state of nature as the context of our lives, because we conventionally disbelieve in natural limits.

Another problem is that there is a considerable overlap between this archetypal story and the pastoral tradition. In the pastoral tradition, as Shakespeare was fully aware, there is a prominent strain of frivolity. What is frivolous is the sentimentalization of rural life, which is supposedly always pretty, pleasant, and free of care. The famous example is Christopher Marlowe's:

> Come live with me and be my love,
> And we will all the pleasures prove
> That valleys, groves, hills, and fields,
> Woods, or steepy mountains yields.

To this Sir Walter Raleigh justly and just as famously replied:

> The flowers do fade, and wanton fields
> To wayward winter reckoning yields . . .

What neither poet acknowledged is the possibility of a real need, as Robert Frost put it, "of being versed in country things."

Shakespeare knew of course the pastoral conventions represented by Marlowe's poem. But he was a countryman, and he knew the truth of Raleigh's admonition; he knew also the need of being versed in country things. He knew that "a true laborer" might have something to say to a courtier that the courtier might need to hear—because, for one reason, the courtier lives by eating country things.

Another obstacle between modern readers and the archetypal story underlying these plays is our popular, and uncritical, egalitarianism. To us, the order of the natural world is horizontal, and so, we would like to think, is the order of human society: Any creature is as important as any other; any citizen is as important as any other.

But to Shakespeare the order of the world, as of human society, is also vertical and hierarchical. The order of created things descends in a Chain of Being from God down to the simplest organisms. In human society, order descends downward from the monarch. Every creature and every human has a place in this hierarchy according to "degree." Ulysses' discourse on degree in the first act of *Troilus and Cressida* can serve as a clarifying prologue to a reading of *As You Like It* and *King Lear*:

> O, when degree is shaked,
> Which is the ladder of all high designs,
> The enterprise is sick. How could communities,
> Degrees in schools, and brotherhoods in cities,
> Peaceful commerce from dividable shores,
> The primogenity and due of birth,
> Prerogative of age, crowns, sceptres, laurels,

But by degree, stand in authentic place?

. . . . . . . . . . . . . . . . . . . .

                  right and wrong,
Between whose endless jar justice resides,
Should lose their names, and so should justice too;
Then everything include itself in power,
Power into will, will into appetite.
And appetite, an universal wolf,
So doubly seconded with will and power,
Must make perforce an universal prey
And last eat up himself.

This speech, by which Ulysses calls the "tortive and errant" Greeks to order, tells us precisely how to understand Orlando's complaint at the beginning of *As You Like It*. Orlando's oldest brother Oliver, charged by their father, now dead, with Orlando's education, has forsaken his duty. Orlando's "keeping," he says to his old servant Adam, "differs not from the stalling of an ox."[1] As the younger brother, lacking the "primogenity . . . of birth," Orlando is a man of lower degree than Oliver. But he is, even so, a man, his father's son, and Oliver's brother; Oliver's mistreatment of him, as if he were no more than a beast, is an affront to order, both human and natural; it is a symptom of a sick enterprise.

The trouble, for Oliver as for the villains of *King Lear* and other Shakespearean villains, is that the human place in the order of things, between the angels and the animals, is precisely and narrowly delimited, and it is precarious. To fall from one's rightful place, to become less than human, is not to become an animal; it

---

1. Quotations are from *As You Like It* (Pelican Shakespeare), ed. Frances E. Dolan (New York: Penguin Group, 2000).

is to become monstrous. And so Oliver's mere dislike and neglect of Orlando decline fairly predictably to a plot to kill him, which forces Orlando into exile.

In scene iii of Act I, a parallel estrangement occurs. The scene is in the palace of Duke Frederick, who has usurped the place of his brother, the carelessly named Duke Senior. Duke Senior, as we have already learned, is in exile in the Forest of Arden where he and some "merry men," his followers, "live like the old Robin Hood of England." Duke Senior's daughter, Rosalind, has been permitted to remain in the palace as the companion of Celia, Duke Frederick's daughter. The two young women not only are cousins and companions but are dearest friends. The two, Celia says are "coupled and inseparable." She says to Rosalind, "Thou and I am one." And it is Celia also who, in attempting to console Rosalind, states one of the main themes common to this play and *King Lear*, that of affection or gentleness or generosity versus force: "what he [her father] hath taken away from thy father perforce, I will render thee again in affection." This affection is soon tested by Duke Frederick's determination to send Rosalind into exile:

> Within these ten days if that thou beest found
> So near our public court as twenty miles,
> Thou diest for it.

His reason is that he does not trust her. His distrust originates of course in his knowledge that he himself is not trustworthy. His daughter and niece, by contrast, possess in full the trust and the trustworthiness now lacking in the court, and so they must leave. In proof both of their friendship and of Duke Frederick's failure to know them, they decide to disguise themselves as "Ganymede" and "Aliena" and run away to join Duke Senior in Arden.

Act II, I think, is the paramount act of the play and is one of the greatest acts in all of Shakespeare. Both its poetry and its drama are exceedingly fine. It is also the crisis of the play for its readers, who have to decide here whether or not to take the play seriously. From what I have read and seen, some readers and directors have found it easy to understand the play as a pastoral diversion, merely sentimental and "comic," which I think is an insult to the play and its poet.

The test comes immediately with Duke Senior's speech that begins the first scene of Act II. The speech develops a standard pastoral theme: the honesty of the pastoral or rural life in contrast to life at court; it is the same theme expounded by Meliboe in *The Faerie Queene*, VI. The duke asks rhetorically, "Are not these woods / More free from peril than the envious court?" And we know the answer as well as his fellow exiles: These woods are free from the envy, jealousy, hypocrisy, power-hunger, and fraud that imperil the court or any other center of power.

There is an editorial crux in line five that we have to settle before reading further. The duke says, "Here feel we not [or: but] the penalty of Adam . . ." I am quoting the new Pelican edition, in which the editor chooses "not." But that usage, if it stands, reduces the speech to nonsense, and the duke to a fool. The problem with this reading is that the duke is *not* a fool, and the exiles, according to the play, are still subject to the penalty of Adam—that is, to mortality, discord, and the need to earn their living. And so the line necessarily is "Here feel we *but* the penalty of Adam . . ." The intended contrast is not between Eden and the fallen world, but between the unadorned life of the forest and the "painted pomp" of the court.

That "the icy fang / And churlish chiding of the winter's wind" are not flatterers but "feelingly persuade me what I am" we may take without argument to be merely true. "Sweet are the uses of adversity" may oversweeten the point, and yet we know that adversity can be corrective, and is sometimes indispensably so.

For modern readers, the largest difficulty in this speech may come in the last three lines, in which the duke proclaims that

> this our life, exempt from public haunt,
> Finds tongues in trees, books in the running brooks,
> Sermons in stones, and good in everything.

To the modern ear, this is likely to sound naive—an instance of the "pathetic fallacy," an almost cartoonish sentimentalization of nature. And yet this is a play solidly biblical and Christian in its moral basis, and this is one of its passages that most insistently depends on our knowledge of scripture. The overarching concept is that of the "good in everything," and the authority for this is Genesis 1:31: "And God saw every thing that he had made, and, behold, it was very good."[2] As for "tongues in trees, books in the running brooks, / Sermons in stones," Shakespeare may be paraphrasing Job 12:7–9:

> Aske now the beastes, and they shal teache thee, and the
>     foules of the heaven, and they shal tel thee:
> Or speake to the earth, and it shal shewe thee: or the fishes
>     of the sea, and they shal declare unto thee.
> Who is ignorant of all these, but that the hand of the Lord
>     hathe made these?

2. All scriptural quotations are from the Geneva Bible.

And he could as well be alluding to the long tradition in which nature is seen as a second or supplementary revelation.

The third scene of Act II parallels thematically the third scene of Act I. In the earlier scene Rosalind is confronted by Duke Frederick, sentenced to exile, and she and Celia make their plan to escape together in disguise. In II, iii, Adam, a servant loyal to Orlando, warns his young master that he, like Rosalind, must go into exile, for his envious and vengeful brother is plotting to kill him.

This play is not an allegory, but some of its characters have a semiallegorical or representative function; they represent human qualities or kinds. Adam, for one, is "the old Adam," father of us all, the fallen humanity which we all share, but he is furthermore the old Adam redeemed by good and faithful service to his master. He was first the servant of Orlando's father, the good Sir Rowland de Boys. In this scene, out of loyalty to the father and love for the son, he makes an absolute gift of his service and his fortune to Orlando, trusting that in his old age he will be comforted by him "that doth the ravens feed" and "caters for the sparrow." Thus, as a true servant to good men, he understands himself as a true servant of God. Orlando reciprocates by saying, like Celia in Act I, that the two of them will join their fates: "we'll go along together" in the belief that, before they have spent all of Adam's savings, they will "light upon some settled low content." The idea of a "settled low content" is the moral baseline of the play. It is what human beings most authentically have a right to expect and to achieve. It is the possibility that adversity most usefully and sweetly reveals. A settled low content is what Thomas Jefferson wished for America's small farmers; it is what Henry Thoreau was seeking at Walden Pond.

In scene iv, having arrived in the Forest of Arden, Rosalind and Celia encounter two other representative figures: Silvius, the young shepherd, and the old shepherd Corin. Silvius, classically named, represents what is most artificial in literary pastorals. He is an "uncouth swain" stricken by love into utter silliness and uselessness; wherever his sheep are, he is not going to think of them during this play.

Corin, by contrast as Englishly named as Spenser's Colin Clout or Hardy's Hodge, is strongly drawn as an individual and at the same time as a representative countryman. He is an "ideal character" of the same honest family as Chaucer's Plowman, who was "A trewe swinkere and a good . . ." Another critical question that this play imposes on its readers and directors is what to make of Corin. Here I have to depart from the sequence of the action to quote Corin's characterization of himself to Touchstone in III, ii:

> Sir, I am a true laborer; I earn that I eat, get that I wear, owe no man hate, envy no man's happiness, glad of other men's good, content with my harm; and the greatest of my pride is to see my ewes graze and my lambs suck.

To many readers that last clause would seem fatally countrified; from them the best rating it could hope for would be "quaint." Many Americans now would see this speech unhesitatingly as the utterance of a "hick" or a "redneck," hopelessly "retro." Nevertheless, any husbander of livestock would recognize Corin as a good shepherd, and Thomas Jefferson would have appraised him highly. In his independence he is democratic, and in his charity, fortitude, and humility he is Christian. Shakespeare knew that the human world survives by the work and responsibility of such people, and Corin's character is one of the standards by which we are to measure the other persons of the play.

In II, iv, Touchstone, assuming the role of sophisticated urbanite, sees Corin on their first encounter as a hick and addresses him accordingly: "Holla, you clown!" But Rosalind, as Ganymede, displaying her extraordinary good sense, recognizes him immediately for what he is: "Good even to you, friend." And Corin replies with perfect courtesy: "And to you, gentle sir, and to you all." Corin, offering hospitality to the strangers, is obliged to reveal that he is poorly paid:

> I am shepherd to another man
> And do not shear the fleeces that I graze.
> My master is of a churlish disposition
> And little recks to find the way to heaven
> By doing deeds of hospitality.

This ungenerous master, moreover, is preparing to sell his flock and land. Rosalind and Celia arrange with Corin to buy "the cottage, pasture, and the flock," Celia promising, "we will mend thy wages." Receiving gratefully this offer of economic justice, Corin sounds again the play's theme of the good servant: "I will your very faithful feeder be . . ."

A fourth representative character is Jaques, whose dominant trait is self-indulgence. "The melancholy Jaques," as he is called in Act II, scene i, manages to be both sentimental and cynical. He is uselessly sensitive and intellectual, a dilettante of his own moods, a boastfully free-speaking critic who corrects nothing. In II, i, Duke Senior speaks of his proper regret at having to kill the deer of the forest for food. But Jaques, as his fellows report, sentimentalizes this regret, making the same equation between human beings and animals as some animal rights advocates of our own day. And, like them, he offers no practicable alternative.

In II, v, after Amiens has sung a song that closely paraphrases Duke Senior's speech in II, i, Jaques responds by supplying a verse of his own which suggests that the forest company are asses and fools. So far he has been a peripheral character, looking on and commenting from the margin as a sort of fecklessly disapproving "chorus." Presently he will serve the play much more vitally, though still passively.

The next scene is brief, containing only two speeches, but to fail to take it seriously enough is again to be seriously in error about the play. Old Adam, weakened by hunger, cannot go on: "Here lie I down and measure out my grave. Farewell, kind master." As a "fallen" man, Adam cannot save himself. Nor can he survive as the servant of Orlando. But *As You Like It* is a play of transformations, and this scene presents the first one. Adam has completed his servanthood. As a servant, he knows, he is as good as dead. His life now depends upon a change in Orlando. And Orlando changes; he becomes his servant's servant—as Edgar in *King Lear*, his father being reduced to helplessness, becomes his father's parent. Shakespeare is relying again on our knowledge of scripture, and the reference here is to Matthew 20:25–27:

> Ye knowe that the lords of the Gentiles have domination over them, and they that are great, exercise autoritie over them.
> But it shall not be so among you: but whosoever wil be great among you, let him be your servant . . .

The apparent lightheartedness of Orlando's reply must be understood as tenderness: as his attempt to lighten the heart of old Adam and as his pledge of service. His words also recall the measure of a "settled low content":

Live a little, comfort a little, cheer thyself a little . . .
For my sake be comfortable; hold death awhile at the
arm's end. I will here be with thee presently, and if I
bring thee not something to eat, I will give thee leave
to die . . .

Here as elsewhere, and despite his allegiance to "degree," there is a
strong democratic impulse in Shakespeare. But he is a democrat,
not in the fashion of Jefferson, but in the fashion of Christ. "The
least of these my brethren" also have their place in the order of
things and their entitlement to be loved and served.

What is the relevance of this to the archetypal story that is my
interest? Let us remember, to start with, that this play begins after
the old state of things, the old "power structure," has fallen. We
don't know what the error or fault of Duke Senior might have
been; we know only that he became so weakened—perhaps so misled by flattery—that he was driven into exile by his power-hungry
brother. Also the good Sir Rowland de Boys has died, and has been
replaced by his selfish eldest son, Oliver. There is nothing more
disorderly and disordering in civilized life than the selfishness of
people of power—that is, their failure to be servants either to God
or to their subjects. ("Public servants," as they and we too often
forget, are meant not to rule but to serve the people.) The corrective to this is begun in the exiles by their recognition of the need
to serve. And, in exile, this need is insistently practical. Outcasts in
the forest—or on the stormy heath—cannot survive by selfishness.

In the long seventh and final scene of Act II, the theme of the forest (or adversity) as the corrective of selfishness and misrule, the

theme of the necessity of servanthood, and the theme of affection or gentleness versus force are all joined in the play's moral climax. In my opinion, this scene threatens also to be the play's dramatic climax—to be both more dramatic and more moving than anything in the three acts that follow. Shakespeare's problem (and I assume a director's also) is to make the rest of the play worthy in moral interest and drama of what he has done in the first two acts.

The seventh scene begins with a leisurely, bantering conversation at first about Jaques and then between Jaques and Duke Senior. Jaques, having encountered Touchstone in the forest, wishes that he too could be a fool, apparently without in the least suspecting that he already is one. If, he says, he were given the liberty of a fool—that is, if the duke should grant him an official tolerance, permitting him to speak the truth as he sees it—then he would prove himself so purgative a critic as to "Cleanse the foul body of th' infected world . . ." The duke says that as such a critic Jaques would necessarily be a hypocrite, "For thou thyself hast been a libertine . . ." Jaques thereupon discourses on the universality of sin and hypocrisy in a speech that prefigures a much better one by the maddened King Lear.

Jaques' speech is interrupted by the entrance of Orlando with his sword drawn, and the scene then gets serious. Dinner has been laid out in the camp of the exiles, and Orlando is desperately in need of food for Adam and for himself. His sword is drawn because, like Touchstone in his encounter with Corin, he is mistaken about the circumstances. He assumes, as he will presently say, that he is in a "savage" place, and therefore will have to take the food by force. In his own savagery, then, he finds himself comically and wonderfully reproved by the duke in the name of "good manners" and "civility." Having fled from the failed civility

of civilization, he has come into the presence of a civility recon-
stituted in the "savage" forest. Instead of drawing his own sword
to defend his dinner, the duke welcomes Orlando as a guest:

> What would you have? Your gentleness shall force
> More than your force move us to gentleness.
>
> . . . . . . . . . . . . . . . . . . . . . . .
>
> Sit down and feed, and welcome to our table.

Orlando, surprised, acknowledges his error and apologizes. He
and Duke Senior then speak an antiphonal celebration of their
common tradition of charity. Orlando says:

> If ever you have looked on better days,
> If ever been where bells have knolled to church,
> If ever sat at any good man's feast,
> If ever from your eyelids wiped a tear
> And know what 'tis to pity and be pitied,
> Let gentleness my strong enforcement be;
> In the which hope I blush, and hide my sword.

And the duke replies:

> True is it that we have seen better days,
> And have with holy bell been knolled to church,
> And sat at good men's feasts, and wiped our eyes
> Of drops that sacred pity hath engendered;
> And therefore sit you down in gentleness,
> And take upon command what help we have
> That to your wanting may be ministered.

But Orlando is not yet ready to sit down. He remains true to his promise to Adam, and he asks the company to "forbear your food a little while . . ." When he speaks of Adam now his kindness is forthright: "like a doe, I go to find my fawn / And give it food." There could be no more tender expression of loving servanthood, and no more apt a simile.

While Orlando is away, Jaques, in response to no encouragement, delivers his famous speech on the seven ages of man. This is a dandy set piece, but it is also utterly cynical. It is the life history of a lone specimen, such as one might find in a modern zoology manual. The last age, which is described most heartlessly,

> Is second childishness and mere oblivion,
> Sans teeth, sans eyes, sans taste, sans everything.

What Shakespeare thought of this may be inferred from the stage direction that immediately follows: "Enter Orlando, with Adam." That Orlando enters carrying Adam in his arms we know from Duke Senior's next speech, which also seems a rebuke to Jaques: "Welcome. Set down your venerable burden / and let him feed." Far from "sans everything," old Adam has a young friend who is his faithful servant—and who moreover, seeing that Adam is in his "second childishness," treats him with a mother's tenderness.

The scene ends with Duke Senior's recognition of Orlando, in which he implicitly affirms love as the right bond between generations and the members of a community: "Be truly welcome hither. I am the duke / That loved your father."

After Act II, *As You Like It* becomes a play of lovers, and the comedy of it, I think, is brilliant enough to follow worthily the eminent scene I have just described. The theme of transformation is worked out in greatest detail and most delightfully in the courtship of Rosalind and Orlando. In this courtship, which is both farcical and serious, Rosalind in the guise of Ganymede assumes the role of "Rosalind," so that Orlando, in the guise of his love-maddened self, may practice as a lover and so be "cured." The premise of this masquerade is set forth by Rosalind in III, ii: "Love is merely a madness . . ." There is good sense in this. She and Orlando fell in love "at first sight" in Act I. Rosalind, who is as smart and resourceful as she needs to be, realizes that such a love requires testing. Lovers in the madness of new love are, as Albany says of Goneril in *King Lear*, "self-covered." Rosalind's "cure," as it turns out, is a trial for herself as well as for Orlando. It removes the "cover" of selfhood; it tests them and proves them worthy of each other and ready for marriage. It is important to notice that these lovers do not turn seriously toward each other and toward their marriage until each of them has explicitly rejected the company of the cynical and sentimental Jaques.

The issue, for Rosalind and for the play, is how to make a civil thing of the wildness of sexual love. The forest is the right place for courtship, which puts lovers in the state of nature. By the same token it is the right place to transform "mad" lovers, if they wish, into grown-up lovers fully prepared for the marriage rite and the "blessed bond of board and bed" with which the play ends.

By the end of the play its "self-covered" villains also have been transformed: Oliver by becoming the conscious and grateful beneficiary of his brother's courage and forgiveness, and Duke Frederick by his encounter with "an old religious man" in "the skirts of this wild wood." Jaques even has resolved to go and learn from "these convertites." Duke Senior and his fellow exiles, as we know from Act II, will return from the forest to a domestic world far better than the one they fled, for they too have been changed, renewed in their specifically human nature, their civility and charity, by this time of adversity in the natural world.

Thus by the play's end all of its principal characters have been changed, and for the better, by their time in the forest. Shakespeare saw, and wants us to see, that the forest can be corrective and restorative to disordered human life. But he goes further. At once explicitly and indirectly he invests the forest with a mysterious and even a mystical transformative power. Partly this is accomplished by Touchstone, speaking with implication apparently beyond his intention. In III, ii, he says to Rosalind, "You have said; but whether wisely or no, let the forest judge." And, twitting Audrey in III, iii, he says, "here we have no temple but the wood . . ." Also Rosalind, in her masquerade with Orlando, alludes to "an old religious uncle of mine" and to "a magician" she has "conversed with." Orlando, in V, iv, conflates the two when he speaks of Ganymede's uncle,

> Whom he reports to be a great magician,
> Obscurèd in the circle of this forest.

Is there, then, a great magician in the forest? Is the forest a holy place of judgment and magical or miraculous transformation? We must ask, but we must not answer. The play must not answer. *As You Like It* is not the voice out of the whirlwind. Once upon a time several people fled from a disordered and murderous society into a forest, and there they were profoundly changed. That is all we know.

## II.

In *King Lear*, both the Lear story and the Gloucester story grow out of corruption at the center of wealth and power, just as does the action of *As You Like It*. Initially, in *King Lear*, this is the corruption merely of selfishness: self-complacency, self-indulgence, self-ignorance, the lack of critical self-knowledge. From this selfishness grows, in turn, an infection of monstrous proportions that is described, though unwittingly, by Gloucester's bastard son, Edmund, in Act I, scene ii, as he works his deception upon Edgar, his legitimate elder brother:

> . . . unnaturalness between the child and the parent; death, dearth, dissolutions of ancient amities; divisions in state, menaces and maledictions against king and nobles; needless diffidences, banishment of friends, dissipation of cohorts, nuptial breaches . . . [3]

Because Lear is king, his self-absorption becomes in effect state policy. Like any head of state he is able, temporarily, to invest his fantasies with power. His fantasy is a primitive instance of "early retirement." He believes that by dividing his kingdom among his daughters he can free himself of care and responsibility while retaining the initiative and the privileges of his kingship. This will prove to be almost limitlessly foolish. He is an "idle old man," as his daughter Goneril calls him, "That still would manage those authorities / That he hath given away." His daughter Regan also is right when she says of him that "he hath ever but slenderly known

---

3. Quotations are from *King Lear* (Pelican Shakespeare), ed. Stephen Orgel (New York: Penguin Group, 1999).

himself." Because he does not know himself, he cannot know others. He has failed disastrously to know Goneril and Regan. He fails to learn of them in the play's first scene what is obvious to everybody else: that they are eloquent, clever, heartless, false, and greedy.

Having apparently determined already the portions of land that he will give to his daughters, Lear involves them pointlessly and cruelly in a contest in which they are to compete for his "largest bounty" by declaring their love for him. Goneril and Regan, good poets and good actors, give him precisely the groveling flattery he has asked for. Only his third daughter, Cordelia, who lacks neither sense nor eloquence, and who in fact truly loves him, refuses to tell him more than the plain truth: She loves him as she ought. She loves him *completely* as she ought, and the play will reveal this, but her refusal to participate in the love contest is entirely proper. It is a refusal to falsify her love by indulging her father's frivolous abuse of his power, which she both disdains and fears.

Predictably infuriated, Lear disinherits Cordelia. In doing so, Martin Lings argues in *The Secret of Shakespeare*, Lear banishes "the Spirit," by which Lings means "the Holy Spirit" or "the pearl of great price." I am unwilling so to allegorize the play, but I think nevertheless that Lings has pointed us in the right direction. In disinheriting Cordelia, in making her "a stranger to my heart and me . . . forever," Lear has, in the face of great evil, estranged himself from goodness. He then deepens and ratifies this estrangement by exiling the Earl of Kent, who has dared to call folly by its right name.

Thus in *King Lear*, exactly as in *As You Like It*, corruption at the center of power sets loose a centrifugal force that ultimately will send the powerless and the defeated into the wildness of the natural world. But in the six or so years between the two plays Shakespeare evidently saw a need to raise the stakes. The archetypal story is, after all, not necessarily a comedy. Selfishness does not necessarily involve one in a limited evil. Evil people are not necessarily relenting or easily converted. The state of nature is not necessarily the relatively hospitable Forest of Arden. The uses of adversity are not necessarily "sweet." The terms and the affirmation of *As You Like It* now required a harsher test.

Shakespeare brought the earlier play to trial by imagining a set of villains who in the course of the play will reveal—and discover for themselves, to their cost—that they have limitlessly consigned themselves to evil. Lacking self-knowledge and too "self-covered" even to suspect that he does, Lear rids his court of love, goodness, and honesty, and thus in effect abandons himself to the purposes of Goneril, Regan, and Regan's husband, the Duke of Cornwall. These three, like Lear, are selfish, but there is a difference. Lear, in his selfishness, is self-deluded: He thinks he is a loving and generous father, as no doubt he wishes to be. Goneril, Regan, and Cornwall, by contrast, are selfish by policy; there is no inconsistency between what they are doing and what they think they are doing. By dividing his kingdom, by isolating himself from Cordelia and Kent, Lear places himself in a deadly trap. Escape will cost him everything he has, or everything he thinks he has in the opening scene. In his quarrel with Kent, he unknowingly foretells his fate: "So be my grave my peace . . ."

In outline, through II, i, the Gloucester story exactly parallels that of Lear. Gloucester has two sons, Edgar and Edmund. Edgar loves his father as Cordelia loves hers. Edmund, the illegitimate younger

son, is as contemptuous of Gloucester as Goneril and Regan are of
Lear. Edmund, like those daughters, is a good actor and flatterer.
He wants to cheat Edgar out of their father's estate, and he suc-
ceeds in convincing Gloucester that Edgar is planning to kill him.
Edgar is then forced to flee to save his own life.

By the beginning of scene iii of Act II, when the fugitive Edgar
transforms himself into Tom o'Bedlam, the villains are successful
and in control; their schemes are working and they have what they
want. Love, goodness, honesty, and fidelity have been directly
confronted by evil, and evil so far has won. But this working of
evil, by its very successes, has instigated a countermovement, and
in parallel to *As You Like It* this movement is the work of good
and faithful servants. The proscriptions against Cordelia, Kent,
and Edgar have set them free to serve Lear and Gloucester.

Disguise in this play is just as important as in *As You Like It*,
and more portentously so. Goneril, Regan, and Cornwall are
"self-covered." Their better selves have been utterly and finally
renounced. Edmund is only barely, but significantly, less self-
obscured than they. Gloucester, like Lear, is a naively selfish old
man. Neither is sinful or evil beyond the measure of ordinary
human behavior, but both are obscured, obscured most conse-
quentially to themselves, by foolishness and complacency. They
are deluded and self-deluded. They are deludable *because* they are
self-deluded. Goneril's husband, the Duke of Albany, for the time
being is disguised to himself because of his hesitancy in recognizing and denouncing the evil character of his wife. In order to
serve Lear and Gloucester in their time of greatest need, Kent and
Edgar must serve in disguise. Of all the major characters, Cordelia alone always appears, to us and to herself, only as she is. She
is good, and her understanding of her goodness is constant, profound, and absolutely assured. Much of the drama and meaning

of the play comes from the actions of the characters in relation to their disguises, and we understand those actions by the measure of Cordelia's transparency, clarity, and candor.

In II, i, the villains of the Lear plot, recognizing their own kind in Edmund, claim him as an ally. Cornwall tells him, with terrible import, "you shall be ours . . . You we first seize on." And so, early in the play, the party of evil, of power-lust and greed, recognizes superficially the usefulness of cooperation, and for a while they are a coherent force. By contrast the party of goodness—the party of Cordelia, Kent, the Fool, Edgar, and, finally, Albany—in its early defeat is widely scattered. As the play proceeds, however, the party of evil, because of the nature of evil, disintegrates while the members of the other party recognize one another and draw together.

Edmund's soliloquy in I, ii, introduces another set of contraries into the play as he subordinates his specifically human nature to nature:

> Thou, Nature, art my goddess; to thy law
> My services are bound. Wherefore should I
> Stand in the plague of custom, and permit
> The curiosity of nations to deprive me,
> For that I am some twelve or fourteen moonshines
> Lag of a brother? Why bastard? Wherefore base . . . ?
> . . . . . . . . . . . . . . . . . . . . . . . . .
> Legitimate Edgar, I must have your land.

If we are fair-minded, we must see the justice of Edmund's indictment of the prejudice against bastards as "base born," just as we see the justice of Goneril and Regan's perception that their father is foolish and intemperate. But evil characteristically supports and disguises itself by such partial claims of justice. In his dire intention to deceive his father and his brother, putting both their lives at risk, Edmund offends against moral law, specifically the fifth, sixth, eighth, ninth, and tenth of the Ten Commandments, and against the order of "degrees" as set forth in Ulysses' speech in *Troilus and Cressida*. Edmund understands "nature" as exclusive self-interest, which he by implication ascribes to all "natural" creatures. As a person self-consciously "enlightened," later in the same scene he rejects his father's astrological determinism, and so accepts full moral responsibility for what he is doing—and again we are tempted to sympathize. But in rejecting his father's superstition, he defines himself as self-determined. By thus subordinating human nature to nature, he means that he accepts *no* subordination. By putting himself at the service of nature's law, he means, perhaps more absolutely than he intends, that he rejects all service to anybody but himself, and will honor *no* law. This speech of Edmund's is answered in IV, vi, by the "Gentleman" who says of Cordelia in an apostrophe to Lear, "Thou hast one daughter / Who redeems nature . . ."

And so the thrusting-out of Lear and Gloucester into the wild world is as profoundly and purposefully thematic in this play as is the forest exile of the sufferers in *As You Like It*. When Lear speaks of Goneril and Regan as "unnatural," he means that they have, like Edmund, subscribed to nature's supposed law of entire selfishness, as opposed to human nature's laws of filiality and love. These virtually opposite uses of the word "nature" may be confusing, but the word in fact has this duplicity in our language, and Shakespeare exploits it fully, to serious purpose, in both plays.

By the unnaturalness of his bad daughters Lear is driven out into nature. Nature now is not the Forest of Arden, but the open heath in the midst of a "pitiless storm." The pitilessness of the storm, which is set before us in its full extremity in the dialogue, is the measure of the pitilessness of Goneril, Regan, and Cornwall— though the pitilessness of the storm, unlike that of these familial villains, is not unkind, as Lear understands and says in III, ii. The heath and the storm belong to the moral landscape of the tragedy, just as the forest belongs to the moral landscape of the comedy. And Lear's dreadful exile upon the heath in the storm and the darkness forces almost immediately a change upon his character. Even as he announces to the Fool that he is going mad—"My wits begin to turn"—he speaks for the first time unselfishly, in compassion and concern for the Fool's suffering: "How dost, my boy? Art cold?" And so his wits are turning, we may say, not just to madness, but through his madness, which is the utter frustration and destruction of his sanity as of Act I, to a better sanity.

Lear's adversity is not "sweet" but it *is* useful: It has made him tender; it has feelingly persuaded him what he is; it has reduced him from a king to a mere human, sharing the lot of other humans. And in III, iv, he speaks in compassion, confession, and repentance, his words recalling both Duke Senior's speech on the uses of adversity and Rosalind and Celia's act of justice toward Corin. These two themes of *As You Like It* recur, with heightened urgency and purpose, in *King Lear*. The disguised Kent, the faithful servant, has led the old king and the Fool to no welcome in Arden, but to a "hovel" that will provide them some meager shelter from the storm. At the doorway Lear says:

> Poor naked wretches, wheresoe'er you are,
> That bide the pelting of this pitiless storm,
> How shall your houseless heads and unfed sides,

> Your looped and windowed raggedness, defend you
> From seasons such as these? O, I have ta'en
> Too little care of this! Take physic, pomp;
> Expose thyself to feel what wretches feel,
> That thou mayst shake the superflux to them
> And show the heavens more just.

Lear's admission, "O, I have ta'en / Too little care of this!" is the turning point of his story. He has heretofore "ta'en care" mainly of himself; that has now become his calamity, and he knows it. His reproof, "Take physic, pomp," recalls Duke Senior's denunciation of "painted pomp" in *As You Like It*, at the same time that it takes up with greater force the earlier play's concern for economic justice. Recognition of the suffering of "Poor naked wretches" leads directly here to the biblical imperative of charity to the poor, for as long as people are painfully in want there is an implicit cruelty in anybody's "superflux" of wealth. This theme is repeated in full by Gloucester in IV, i, after he has given his purse to "Poor Tom":

> Heavens, deal so still!
> Let the superfluous and lust-dieted man,
> That slaves your ordinance, that will not see
> Because he does not feel, feel your pow'r quickly;
> So distribution should undo excess,
> And each man have enough.

In revenge for his kindness and service to the king during the storm, Gloucester has been captured by Cornwall and Regan, who bind him and put out his eyes. He too is then thrust out, blind and (as his tormentors believe) alone, into the world and the weather—to "smell / His way to Dover," as Regan says in as cruel a speech as was ever written.

But immediately after the terrible scene of his blinding, we find that Gloucester is not after all alone. He is helped first by an elderly servant who, in the little he tells of himself, answers exactly to the description of the old Adam of *As You Like It*:

> O my good lord,
> I have been your tenant, and your father's tenant,
> These fourscore years.

And then he is helped by Edgar in the guise of Tom o'Bedlam or Poor Tom, who is in fact his father's faithful servant, guide, and teacher, and who at last "save[s] him from despair."

Cast out into the storm and the darkness, Lear too is accompanied—first by the Fool and then by Kent and then by Gloucester, at what cost we know, and then by Cordelia and Albany. These are the good and faithful servants of this play, and they continue here *As You Like It*'s theme of service and, with it, the earlier play's theme of affection and generosity as opposed to force. But good service in *King Lear* is more costly than in *As You Like It*, also less effective, and thus it emerges in what Shakespeare must have concluded is its true character. Kent is exiled because he understands faithful service, not only as loyalty, as faithful help, but also as truth-telling, requiring even opposition. In this Kent is contrasted with Oswald, who is a bad servant because he connives in the evil of his masters and does as he is told; and Oswald is again contrasted with Cornwall's "First Servant," who opposes his master's cruelty to Gloucester and dies for his insubordination.

By the time he wrote *King Lear*, Shakespeare clearly had begun to doubt that it is possible to consent to use by policy a little or a limited evil to serve some perceived "good," and then to stop before the evil has enlarged to some unforeseen perfection of itself. This perfection, as Shakespeare saw it, was the destruction of the evildoers along with whatever else might be destroyed by them. (This is the tragedy itself of *Macbeth*, which was written in the next year.)

Self-destruction, after selfishness has been accepted as a policy, is merely a matter of logic, as explained in Ulysses' speech. The key insight is given by Cornwall in III, vii, when, before the blinding of Gloucester, he speaks of "our wrath, which men / May blame, but not control"; and again by Goneril in V, iii: "the laws are mine ..." If the laws belong to individual persons—if Goneril, as queen, does not rule "under the law"—then those persons are in effect lawless. The party of evil is by definition out of control from the start. Its members are out of control as individuals dedicated to self-interest. People who are united by the principle of unrestrained self-interest have inevitably a short-lived union. However large and however costly to their victims their successes may be, their failure is assured. But their espousal of evil as a deliberate policy assures also that they will be unrelenting while they last.

To this great force of relentless if self-doomed evil Shakespeare opposes the counterforce of good and faithful service. As Lear and Gloucester are made powerless, poor, and helpless, the theme of help manifests itself in the presence and the acts of people entirely dedicated to serving them. But Lear and Gloucester in their selfishness are too vulnerable, and the wickedness of their adversaries is too great, to permit to the good servants any considerable practical success. They can give no victory and achieve no restoration, as the world understands such things. Their virtues do not lead certainly or even probably to worldly success, as some bad teachers would have us believe. They stand by, suffering what they cannot help, as parents stand by a dying or disappointing child. This assures only the survival in this world of faithfulness, compassion, and love—which is no small thing.

But this play refuses to stop at what the world understands of service or success. For Lear and Gloucester worldly failure is fully assured; it is too late for worldly vindication. What the good servants can do, and this they succeed in doing, is restore those defeated old men to their true nature as human beings. They can waken them to love and save them from despair.

It is obvious by now that I have begun to argue against what we might call the "dark interpretation" of *King Lear*. The dark interpretation is well represented by Stephen Orgel, editor of the new Pelican edition of "the traditional conflated text," who sums the meaning of the play as follows:

> The world is an instrument of torture, and the only comfort is in the nothing, the never, of death. The heroic vision is of suffering, unredeemed and unmitigated.

It is impossible to see this nihilistic reading of the play as valid, and hard to see it as "heroic." There is a kind of modern mind that finds Hell more imaginable and believable than Heaven and nihilism more palatable than redemption. What is "heroic" to this mind is the "courage" to face the immitigable pointlessness of human experience. This is the same mind that, in default of any structure of meaning, finds all bad outcomes, political or economic or ecological, to be "inevitable."

Before even approaching the issues of this play's ending, one ought at least to consider the biblical context within which Shakespeare oriented his work. *King Lear* was written in reference to three passages in the Gospel of Matthew. Like *As You Like It*, it alludes repeatedly, and more insistently and sternly, to the call to service in Matthew 20 that I quoted earlier. And more forcibly than in the earlier play it extends the obligation of service to "the least of these my brethren" (Matthew 25:40), for who more than Lear and Gloucester in their injury and helplessness could be counted as "least"? And unlike the comedy, the tragic play broods constantly on the idea, in Matthew 10:39 and also in the other three Gospels, of losing one's life in order to find it. This theme is stated plainly in II, i, when the King of France says to Cordelia, "Thou losest here, a better where to find," and this strikes so nearly to the heart of the play as to be virtually its subject.

In I, iv, Kent, newly exiled and in disguise, his old life thus lost, says to himself:

> If thou canst serve where thou dost stand condemned,
> So may it come thy master whom thou lov'st
> Shall find thee full of labors.

This is a literal description of Kent's predicament in the play, if we read "thy master" as King Lear, and "condemned" as Kent's exile. But it is also, and just as literally, a description of the human predicament and consequent obligation, if we read "thy master" as Christ, and "where thou dost stand condemned" as the fallen world.

In III, iv, Edgar as Poor Tom, in his feigning madness, recites a number of pertinent biblical laws, four of them from the Ten Commandments.

In IV, ii, when Albany says to Goneril, "Wisdom and goodness to the vile seem vile . . . ," Shakespeare could be recalling
Isaiah 5:20: "Wo unto them that speake good of evil, and evil of
good . . ."

Cordelia's sentence, lines 23–24 in IV, iv, has the same ambigu-
ity as Kent's speech cited earlier: "O dear father, / It is thy business
I go about." This either is an apostrophe to Lear or it is a prayer
recalling Luke 2:49, in which Jesus says to his parents, "knewe ye
not that I must go about my fathers busines?"

In IV, vi, when Edgar, seeing Lear in his madness "bedecked with
weeds," exclaims, "O thou side-piercing sight!" he is recalling John
19:34: "But one of the soldiers with a spear pierced his side . . ."

When Lear in his mad sermon in IV, vi, says, "See how yond justice rails upon yond simple thief. Hark in thine ear: change places
and, handy-dandy, which is the justice, which is the thief?" his
words paraphrase Romans 2:1: "Therefore thou art inexcusable,
o man, whosoever thou art that judgest: for in that thou judgest
another, thou condemnest thy self: for thou that judgest, doest
the same things."

Gloucester's prayer in the same scene—

> You ever-gentle gods, take my breath from me;
> Let not my worser spirit tempt me again
> To die before you please

—is the daunting submission of the Lord's Prayer and of Christ's
agony in Gethsemane: "Thy wil be done . . ."

Cordelia's lamentation over her father in IV, vii—". . . and wast
thou fain, poor father, / To hovel thee with swine and rogues forlorn . . ."—recalls the story of the Prodigal Son. She wakens Lear
a few lines later in what he perceives as a resurrection. And her

forgiveness of his offenses against her—"No cause, no cause"—is Christ's: not a mere human excusing or overlooking of an error, but the cancellation of its cause in Lear's fallen nature; his wrong no longer exists to be forgiven.

The trumpets that sound in V, iii, must have sounded in Shakespeare's imagination, and to the ears of many in his audiences, like the trumpets of Revelation, for they are a summoning to judgment.

When Albany in V, iii, offers to "friends . . . / The wages of their virtue," the words evoke Romans 6:23: "For the wages of sinne is death; but the gifte of God is eternal life . . ."

And when Kent, in his final speech, says, "My master calls me; I must not say no," he is confirming earlier suggestions of his impending death. But here we have again that term "master," which in I, iv, we could take to be ambiguous, but which here we are bound to understand as referring to Christ. To assume that "master" refers to Lear is to assume that Kent thinks Lear will require his services in the hereafter, a sentimentality that puts Kent far out of character.

The play, furthermore, contains three references to the miraculous, always in circumstances of great misery, reminding us that Christ's miracles are almost always performed on behalf of those who are seemingly beyond help. Kent, in the stocks in II, ii, says, "Nothing almost sees miracles / But misery." And Edgar, after Gloucester's "suicide" in IV, vi, says to him in the playacting of his "cure," but in fact urging the realization on him: "Thy life's a miracle." A few lines further on, he says, "the clearest gods who make them honors / Of men's impossibilities have preserved thee."

The foregoing list of biblical references may be incomplete or otherwise at fault. But it is at least sufficient to show that Shakespeare thought of the action of this play as occurring in a context far larger than that of what we have come to mean by "realism."

❧

Anybody looking for meaninglessness or nihilism in *King Lear* can find it in abundance, but nearly all of it is in the deeds and the implicit principles of the villains. There are, however, three statements in the play that are explicitly and pointedly nihilistic.

The first is in one of Lear's speeches in III, iv, when in the storm he is reduced, as he thinks, virtually to nothing, and in his madness he adopts a fierce reductionism of his own. "Is man no more than this?" he asks of the nearly naked Edgar. And then, addressing Edgar, he says, "Thou art the thing itself; unaccommodated man is no more but such a poor, bare, forked animal as thou art." This, now under the weight of tragedy, is Jaques' conclusion in his "seven ages" speech; "unaccommodated man" is a lone specimen "sans everything."

A considerable part of the purpose of this play is to answer such statements, and this one is answered simply by the circumstances in which it is uttered. Lear's despair at this point is over the failure of a mere man to be successfully selfish. He cannot secure for himself his own wishes, and he cannot, alone, save himself even from the weather. But as bad as his predicament is, as nearly hopeless as it is, he is not "unaccommodated." Like the old Adam of *As You Like It*, he is not alone. Kent, the Fool, and Edgar are with him. A little later Gloucester enters with a torch to offer what help he can. With one most consequential exception, the good people of the play are going to be with him, doing all they can for him, to the end. What they can do is not enough, but they stand nonetheless for all that is opposite to his trouble and his suffering, his rage and his despair. They stand for the faithfulness that is opposed to treachery and the gentleness that is opposed to force.

The second expression of utter despair needing some comment is blinded Gloucester's accusation against "th' gods" in IV, i. This phrase "th' gods" is in keeping with a parliamentary proscription of the use of the word "God" on the stage, which the Puritans thought to be blasphemous. And so Gloucester was reduced to blaming the Greek and Roman deities: "As flies to wanton boys are we to th' gods; / They kill us for their sport."

Gloucester says this just after he has met Edgar-as-Poor-Tom. From now until Gloucester's death, Edgar's ruling purpose is to save his father from despair. Gloucester's sentence, while avoiding the appearance of blasphemy so fearful to the Puritan politicians, is authentically blasphemous, as Edgar understands. It is blasphemous, desperate, and perfectly self-centered. It is self-pity in extremis, driving him to say what he can hardly bear to say and cannot know. To save him from despair is to save him from the death of "a poor, bare, forked animal" reduced to the self-indulgence of self-pity. And by the end of the Gloucester story Edgar has led his father to a proper care for his life ("Thy life's a miracle") and to the proper submission to divine will that I quoted earlier. Edgar's service to Gloucester is clearly to be understood as redemptive, and he is not being frivolous when he says that his father died "smilingly" between the two extremes of "joy and grief."

My final exhibit in this line of nihilism is from a speech of Edmund's. Near the end of the play he sends a "captain" to follow Lear and Cordelia to prison, with instructions to kill them. Here is his justification: "Know thou this, that men / Are as the time is." This is a crude, self-serving determinism, the counterpart of "It is inevitable." All the energy and passion of *King Lear* gathers to refute this speech. *Some* men are as the time is, some always are, and they have always said so in self-justification. But Cordelia is not as the time is, Kent is not, Edgar is not, Albany is not, even the Fool is not.

And so these three assertions of hopelessness and meaninglessness are answered with three resounding nos that are passionately affirmative: No, "unaccommodated man" is not the type specimen of humanity. No, you are not eligible to conclude that the gods kill us for their sport. No, all men are not "as the time is."

By the end of the play we can have no doubt that we have watched a deadly skirmish in the battle between good and evil. We have watched the passage of tormented souls and a human community through a profound disorder, in which they have been driven away from their comforts and customary assurances into the world's unaccommodating wildness. The consequences of this casting out are surely tragic and horrifying. The death of Cordelia, as Dr. Johnson and others have testified, is shocking; it is nearly unbearable. The survivors are clearly in shock themselves, barely able to speak. And so we now must ask if in fact *King Lear* conforms to the archetypal story I outlined at the beginning. Are Lear and Gloucester in any sense reformed or redeemed by their great suffering? Is there any promise of a return to civil order? Does the play (to quote J. A. Bryant Jr.) "satisfy the society's impulse to renewal"?

Well, before concluding with the proponents of darkness that the play merely demonstrates the meaninglessness of suffering, we need to deal patiently with certain facts. The first of these is that by the play's end every one of the villains is dead—and not one of them is dead by chance. The death of each has come as a logical consequence of the assumption that human nature can be satisfactorily subordinated to nature. This assumption has proved to be as uncontrollable as the storm on the heath. There is a right relation between nature and human nature, and to get it wrong is eventually to perish. Shakespeare does not present this as an issue of justice, for such wrongs may destroy the innocent as well as the guilty; he presents it as the natural result of unnatural (that is, inhuman) behavior. The conflict of the two natures is revealed in Edmund's dying effort to redeem himself: "Some good I mean to do, / Despite of mine own nature."

According to this view, it would be too much to expect a "comic" outcome, for great evil will victimize the good. But the good people, unlike the evil ones, are not inevitably destroyed. Another fact is that, as the play ends, Kent, Edgar, and Albany are still alive. Kent's life is in doubt, but Edgar and Albany are young and will live on. In them is a reasonable hope for the restoration of civil order. And not only have those three survived, but in the course of the play, together with Cordelia and the Fool, they have grown ever greater in our respect and love, as has Shakespeare himself for imagining such people.

Another fact hard to ignore is the work of forgiveness. Both Cordelia and Edgar freely forgive their erring fathers, and by this forgiveness those fathers are made more truly and fully human.

Now we must deal with the reconciliation of the two plots. This is not really a problem, except that it has been made so by bad reading. The "problem" for the dark interpreter is that the Lear and the Gloucester stories are parallel, each enlarging our understanding of the other by resonating with it. The "problem" is that the Gloucester story is explicitly redemptive, for Edgar intends, as he says, to save his father from despair, and he succeeds, whereas the Lear story, according to the dark interpretation, ends in despair:

"suffering, unredeemed and unmitigated." How can a play thus have two plots and two meanings that absolutely contradict each other and still deserve our respect? Stephen Orgel solves this problem by asserting that "Gloucester is effectively abandoned by the play." But this only raises a worse problem: Why would Shakespeare have given so much of his play, and so much magnificent poetry, to a secondary plot that he later "abandons"? And why should we indulge or forgive his doing so?

Another, more sensible way to deal with the supposed problem is to ask if Lear's story actually ends in despair, and thus in contradiction of Gloucester's story. To answer, we must look with the greatest care at Lear's final speech. It is possible, I suppose, to read or speak those lines as an unpausing scramble of outrage, grief, and despair. But the speech in fact has five parts, involving four profound changes of mind and mood. It begins with a complaint:

And my poor fool is hanged: no, no, no life?

This is tenderness, heartbreaking enough, but it bears still a taint of the old selfishness. Cordelia is "*my* poor fool." Her death here is perceived as Lear's loss, not hers. Then comes a natural outrage:

Why should a dog, a horse, a rat, have life,
And thou no breath at all?

All grief over the death of the young, especially the death of one's own child, must bear the burden of such a question. And only after that ineluctable and futile question, which also comes from his own loss, can Lear turn his thoughts fully to the dead girl in his arms, and, forgetting himself, speak to her of her death:

Thou'lt come no more,
Never, never, never, never, never.

And then, turning to one of the bystanders, he says:

Pray you undo this button. Thank you, sir.

This is literally meant. His clothes are somehow binding; he asks and receives help with a button. But the button is symbolic as well; it, or this small discomfort, is the last thing holding him to the world. This is not the renunciation of Gloucester's "suicide," but rather a profound submission and relinquishment of his will. At this point all the emotions of the preceding lines, and of his tragedy, pass from him, with the result that at last he *sees* Cordelia:

Do you see this? Look on her! Look, her lips,
Look there, look there—

Martin Lings, in *The Secret of Shakespeare*, understands Lear's story as at once a descent into Hell and a Purgatory, and he thinks that when Lear speaks these final two lines he is seeing Cordelia again, and this time in truth, as "a soul in bliss." I have no doubt that the play can be read or presented as Dr. Lings suggests. And yet I hesitate. The difficulty is that Shakespeare, as it seems to me, was not a visionary Christian; he was not Dante. The redemption he saw as possible for Gloucester and Lear did not come by way of an intercession from Heaven. It was earned, or lived out, or suffered out, in an unrelenting confrontation both with the unregenerate self, the self-covered self, and with the deliberate evil of others. The straight way was lost to Gloucester and Lear as it was to Dante, but it was recoverable to them by a self-loss more painful, and nearer too late, than Dante's.

I am content to rest with the more literal understanding that Cordelia, the play's only wholly undisguised character, has been disguised to Lear until the end by his self-preoccupying pride, anger, outrage, guilt, grief, and despair; and that, when his vision clears at last and he can see her as she was and is, he is entirely filled with love and wonder. And so the play may be said to show us at last a miracle: that Lear, dying, is more alive than he has ever been until this moment.

# God, Science, and Imagination

~

(2008)

Among the oddest bedevilers of our time are the eminent scientists who use their heaped-up credentials, achievements, and awards as pedestals from which to foretell the future and pronounce upon the ultimate questions of life and religion. One of the most recent of these is Steven Weinberg's essay "Without God" in *The New York Review of Books* for September 25, 2008.

The oddity of these ventures, of which Professor Weinberg's is fairly typical, is in their ready—and, it seems to me, their thoughtless—abandonment of scientific rigor and methodology. For example, despite his protest that he does not want "to try to talk anyone out of their [*sic*] religion," Prof. Weinberg sets forth an elaborate argument for the nonexistence of God, an argument obviously meant to be persuasive but one that is based entirely on opinion.

As a fundamentalist of science, like the fundamentalists of religion, he is clearly evangelizing, hoping to convert or at least to disturb those who disagree. And like the religious fundamentalists, he uses a language that presents belief as knowledge. But more troubling than the authority he grants to his own opinions is his claim to know what cannot be known. "As religious belief weakens," he writes, "more and more of us know that after death there is nothing." The only fact available here is that Prof. Weinberg and more and more of us do not, and will never, know any such thing. There is no proof of this "nothing," and there is no scientific or other procedure by which to attempt such a proof.

Prof. Weinberg is a physicist, and he says that he is "professionally concerned with finding out what is true." But as a mere person he evidently is concerned, like too many others, merely with investing his opinions with power. This is the concern of fundamentalists of all kinds: religious, atheistic, scientific, technological, economic, and political. They all seek power—they seek victory, in fact—by abandoning the proprieties that permit us to seek and to honor what is true while acknowledging the limits of our ability to know.

Not far into his essay, Prof. Weinberg says, with proper humility, "Of course, not everything has been explained, nor will it ever be." But, two paragraphs later, speaking of "religious conservatives," he abandons the careful and exacting speech of humility, and prognosticates with the absolute confidence and gleeful vengefulness of a religious conservative: "I can imagine how disturbed they will feel in the future, when at last scientists learn how to understand human behavior in terms of the chemistry and physics of the brain, and nothing is left that needs to be explained by our having an immaterial soul."

This is something else that he does not know. Nor does he hesitate over the apparent difficulty of a material proof of the nonexistence of something immaterial.

The argument about the existence of God necessarily must be conducted in the absence of evidence that would stand as proof in either a laboratory or a court of law. There is no objective or empirical or experimental evidence on either side. The argument, as such, is by definition hopeless—a piece of foolishness and a waste of time. Even so, it has long existed and no doubt it will long continue, but only for the paltry reason that it cannot be won. Chaucer defined the problem about six hundred years ago, and I doubt that it can be more clearly defined:

> A thousand tymes have I herd men telle
> That ther ys joy in hevene and peyne in helle,
> And I acorde wel that it ys so;
> But, natheles, yet wot I wel also
> That ther nis noon dwellyng in this contree,
> That eyther hath in hevene or helle ybe,
> Ne may of hit noon other weyes witen,
> But as he hath herd seyd, or founde it writen;
> For by assay ther may no man it preve.
> —*The Prologue to the Legend of Good Women*

People of religion, and not just fundamentalists, can speak with tiresome confidence of knowing what in fact they don't know but instead believe. None of us is immune to the temptation to do this. Modern science itself, ignoring its famous devotion to empirical proof and factuality, has pampered and marketed itself by beliefs that have proved to be empirically flimsy and unimaginably damaging. Chemistry, while helping us to "live better," has poisoned the whole world; the "elegant" science of nuclear physics, while making us "safe" from our enemies and offering us "cheap" and "peaceful" power, has littered the world with lethal messes that apparently are irremediable; and so on to genetic engineering and other giddy "miracles." These developments, at least in their origin, are scientific. But the science involved has not been comprehensive or humble or self-critical or neighborly or publicly responsible. Mere self-interest obliges us to doubt the scientific faith that facts alone can assure the proper or safe use of facts. Modern science, as we have known it and as it has represented itself to us, has encouraged a healthy skepticism of everything but itself. But surely it implies no disrespect for science if we regard it with the skepticism upon which it prides itself.

We human beings, because we are short-lived creatures of limited intelligence, are going to remain under the necessity of talking about things that we don't provably know. But respect for "what is true," for what we don't know, and for our neighbors and fellow creatures, requires us to know and to say when we *don't* know.

Prof. Weinberg understands religious belief as "the belief in facts about God or the afterlife." This is a mistake. If "fact" means what we have agreed it means, and if we respect the word, then we have to say with Chaucer that none of us knows any facts about God or the afterlife. If we did, there would be no issue of "belief." We know for sure that it is possible to speak of beliefs and opinions as facts, but that does not make the beliefs and opinions factual; it only makes them lies.

Most writers about religion, however, have not been scientists, or consciously subject to the methodological strictures of science. If they speak of knowledge, they may mean the things one knows from tradition or from unreplicable experience or "from the heart."

Even so, in the Bible the language of belief often falls far short of the confidence of factual knowledge. It is most moving—and, to me, it seems most authentic—when it is honestly confronting its own imperfection, or the inadequacy or failure of knowledge. Far from the cocksureness of fundamentalism, the starting place of authentic belief or faith is not-knowing.

One of the primary characteristics of the biblical God is his irreducibility; he cannot be confined in any structure of human comprehension. And so in 1 Kings, having completed his temple, Solomon cries out, not with confident religiosity, but with despair; his mighty work has contradicted what apparently was its purpose:

> But will God indeed dwell on the earth? behold, the heaven and heaven of heavens cannot contain thee; how much less this house that I have builded? (8:27)

The supplication of Mark 9:24 is likewise authenticated by its honest unknowing, unconfidence, and sense of struggle: "Lord, I believe; help thou my unbelief." And Paul's letter to the Romans is precise and unrelenting in his definition of hope:

> For we are saved by hope: but hope that is seen is not hope: for what a man seeth, why doth he yet hope for? But if we hope for that we see not, then do we with patience wait for it. (8:24–25)

"Faith," at root, is related to "bide" and "abide." It has certainly the sense of belief, but also the sense of difficult belief—of waiting, of patience, of endurance, of hanging on and holding together.

And so Prof. Weinberg's definition of "belief" involves not

only a misuse of the word "facts," but also an implicit misunderstanding of the word "faith."

I dislike very much the disciplinary provincialisms of the universities; therefore, as a literary person, I ought to be delighted that Prof. Weinberg finds literature as irresistible as religion. But I am obliged instead to regret that he speaks of it with complacent oversimplification and ineptitude. When he says, for example, that "nothing prevents those of us who have no religious belief from enjoying religious poetry," does he mean that such enjoyment is the same for believers and unbelievers? If so, how does he know this? Does he have a way of comparing objectively the degrees and kinds of enjoyment? I would gladly agree that enjoyment is a desirable, maybe even a necessary, result of any art; but is enjoyment the only or the highest effect of religious art? What is it about religious art that unbelievers enjoy? The underlying question here, and an important one, is this: How do you authenticate, and make credible to somebody else, your response to a work of art? Prof. Weinberg seems not to have suspected that this question exists, or that it implies a careful, difficult job of work.

He likewise suspects no danger in his assertion that "we see already that little English language poetry written in the past few decades owes anything to belief in God." But who is "we"? How many decades does he have in mind? What is signified by "little"? The existence of God is not a statistical issue to be proved or disproved by quantities of belief or numbers of believers. If God exists, then, like Prof. Weinberg, he exists independently of anybody's knowledge or anybody's belief or disbelief in his existence. If *nobody* believed in God, Prof. Weinberg would still have his case to make, and evidence would be required of him that he cannot produce.

He says further that "very great poetry can be written without religion," using Shakespeare as his example, apparently unaware that Shakespeare's religion is still a controversial issue among Shakespearean scholars. But you don't have to be an expert—you have only to read the Bible and the plays—to know of Shakespeare's frequent allusions to scripture and his concern with scriptural themes such as mercy and forgiveness and with scriptural characters such as the good and faithful servant. But if great poetry can be written without religion, what does that prove about religion? It proves only that great poetry can be written without it.

In the boring, pointless, and destructive quarrel between fundamentalist science and fundamentalist religion, it seems to me that both sides are wrong. The religious fundamentalists are wrong because their disrespect for the materiality of the world involves, as a matter of course, disrespect for material evidence. They are like a jury that sees no significance in a "smoking gun" because its members don't believe in guns or smoke. The fundamentalist scientists are wrong because they counter one absolutism with another. Against their own history and tradition, they assume the posture of absolute certainty and unquestionability. Both sides assume that they are right now and forever. Neither can say "I don't know" or "I wonder." Both are bigoted, unforgiving, and humorless.

In his troubled and consoling last book of poems, *Second Space*, Czeslaw Milosz includes a poem of exemplary generosity:

If there is no God,
Not everything is permitted to man.
He is still his brother's keeper
And he is not permitted to sadden his brother,
By saying there is no God.

This instruction, as Milosz undoubtedly knew, is perfectly reversible: If there is a God, that does not justify condescension or insult to your atheist neighbor. Such differences, so far as I can see, become issues of justice only when one side attempts to abridge or deny the freedom of the other.

If in fact the fundamentalist scientists were as smart as they think they are, and if the religious fundamentalists were as secure in their belief as they claim to be, then they would (except for issues of justice) leave one another in peace. They keep pestering each other because they need each other. The sort of mind that is inclined to fundamentalism is not content within itself or within its own convictions or principles. It needs to humiliate its opponents. It needs the sustenance of converts. It is fundamentally insecure and ungenerous.

Worst of all, the fundamentalists of both science and religion do not adequately understand or respect imagination. Is imagination merely a talent, such as a good singing voice, the ability to "make things up" or "think things up" or "get ideas"? Or is it, like science, a way of knowing things that can be known in no other way? We have much reason to think that it is a way of knowing things not otherwise knowable. As the word itself suggests, it is the power to make us *see*, and to see, moreover, things that without it would be unseeable. In one of its aspects it is the power by which we sympathize. By its means we may see what it was to be Odysseus or Penelope, or David or Ruth, or what it is to be one's neighbor or one's enemy. By it, we may "see ourselves as others see us." It is also the power by which we see the place, the predicament, or the story we are in.

To use what is by now the most notorious example, the creation story in Genesis is neither science nor pseudo-science, neither history nor pseudo-history. Like other traditional creation stories, it welled up out of the oldest, deepest human imagination to help us, even now, to see what it is to have a wondrous world that had a beginning in time. It is not true by the corroboration of contemporary documents or physical evidence. It is the imagination, in the high sense given to it by the greatest poets, that assents to its truth, just as it assents to the story of King Lear or Blake's rendering of Jacob's vision. The following lines, from Hayden Carruth's *Toward the Distant Islands*, rightly ignoring the unwinnable contest of science versus religion, were written with a proper deference to mystery and a proper respect for imagination:

> The *Iliad*, the *Odyssey*, the *Book of Genesis*,
> These were acts of love, I mean deeply felt gestures, which
>         continuously bestow upon us
> What we are.

As for the afterlife, it has been imagined by Homer, Virgil, the biblical writers, Dante, and others, with the result that at least some of us, their willing heirs, have imagined it also.

I don't see that scientists would suffer the loss of any skin from their noses by acknowledging the validity and the power of imaginative truths, which are harmless to the truths of science, even though imagination in the highest sense seems allied less to science than to religion. The first chapters of Genesis are imagined and imaginable, whereas the big bang theory is the result of calculation. If you have read Dante, you can imagine Hell, Purgatory, and Heaven, but reading Prof. Weinberg cannot help you to imagine "nothing."

Perhaps the most interesting thing that Prof. Weinberg says in his essay is this: "There are plenty of people without religious faith who live exemplary moral lives (as for example, me)." This of course is a joke, modeled on the shameless self-commendation of politicians, but it is a joke without a context sufficient to reveal how large and sad a joke it is. The large sad fact that gives the joke its magnitude and its cutting edge is that there is probably not one person now living in the United States who, by a strict accounting, could be said to be living an exemplary moral life.

We are still somewhere in the course of the most destructive centuries of human history. And, though I believe I know some pretty good people whom I love and admire, I don't know one who is not implicated, by direct participation and by proxies given to suppliers, in an economy, recently national and now global, that is the most destructive, predatory, and wasteful the world has ever seen. Our own country in only a few hundred years has suffered the loss of maybe half its arable topsoil, most of its original forest and prairie, much too much of its mineral wealth and underground water. Most of its surface water and all of its air are polluted. Its rural cultures—the cultures, at their best, of husbandry—have been almost annihilated. Many of its plants and animals, both wild and domestic, are extinct or in danger.

It is littered with wastelands, landfills, and, most shameful and fearful of all, dumps, industrial sites, and whole landscapes made dangerous virtually forever by radioactive waste. An immense part of this damage has been done in the years after World War II, when the machinery and chemicals of industrial warfare were turned upon the land—to make production "efficient" by the most doubtful standards and to replace the people of the land economies. I have no doubt that the dualisms of body and soul, heaven and earth, too prominent among the religious, have been damaging both to people and to the world, for that division has made it easy to withhold the necessary protections from material things. But the materialists of the science-technology-industry complex, whose minds are not so divided, and who might have been expected to value highly the material world, have instead held it in contempt and damaged it more than anybody.

Scientists and scholars in the knowledge industry—corporate or academic, if there is a difference—are probably in the greatest moral jeopardy of anybody except political, military, and corporate leaders. All knowledge now is potentially a commodity, and there is no way for its originators to control, or even foresee, the uses to which it may be put.

I would like, in conclusion, to bring up a question of religion and politics that I think needs more attention from everybody, but maybe especially from atheists. Before going on, I had better say that I adhere absolutely to the First Amendment. Any form of religious coercion by religious organizations or by governments would be intolerable to me. The idea of the separation of church and state seems to me fairly clear when it is a matter simply of limiting the powers of institutions. But the world is not so simple as to allow a neat, clear separation of politics and religion or of politics and irreligion.

My question is about the origin and existence of human rights. How did we get them? How are they authenticated? In ancient traditional cultures such as those of surviving peasant or hunter-gatherer communities, the people may be said to possess certain rights by tradition and inheritance: Because they have possessed them immemorially, they possess them still. No modern government, younger and of shallower origin, could rightfully revoke or ignore them. A younger nation of recent immigrants such as the United States possesses no rights by immemorial tradition and inheritance. The founders understood this, and so they stated in our Declaration of Independence the principle that "all men" (which we now construe as "all people") "are endowed by their Creator with certain inalienable Rights."

I don't think it is adequately appreciated how essential, and what a stroke of political brilliance, that statement is. The purport of it is that, as humans, we have rights that precede the existence of any government. We therefore were not on our knees to the government of England then, and we are not kneeling to our own government now, beseeching a grant of rights. As a would-be free people we were, and we are, requiring any government whatever to recognize and honor the rights we have always possessed by divine gift. The difference between rights granted by a government and rights given by "our Creator" is critical, for it is the difference between rights that are absolute and rights that are contingent upon the will or the whim of those in power.

The possession of rights by divine endowment obviously is an article of faith, for it has no objective or empirical standing. It would have no standing at all with a government in principle atheistic. (We had better hope, I think, that the separation of church and state implies the separation of institutional atheism and the state.) But vulnerable as this principle may be as an article merely of faith, I know of no other authorization of human rights that can adequately replace it.

It is easy to anticipate that some who will not allow any validity to divine rights will bring forward "natural rights" as an alternative. But this too would be an article of faith, and it forces upon us the probably unanswerable question of what, in the nature of nature, might bring forth and confer upon us rights specifically human.

I am not able to settle such questions, even to my own satisfaction. And so I am obliged to conclude by offering the possibility that we humans are by definition, and perhaps by nature, creatures of faith (which we are as likely to place in luck or science or the free market or our own intelligence as in some version of God); and that we are further defined by principles and cultural properties, not objectively verifiable, that we inherit.

# Acknowledgments

———————— ❧ ————————

"Imagination in Place" was first published in *Place in American Fiction*, ed. H. L. Weatherby and George Core (Columbia, MO: University of Missouri Press, 2004).

"American Imagination and the Civil War" was first published in *The Sewanee Review*, October–December 2007.

"The Momentum of Clarity" was previously published as "Wallace Stegner and Influence" in *Wallace Stegner: Man & Writer*, ed. Charles E. Rankin (Albuquerque, NM: University of New Mexico Press, 1996), and *Catching the Light: Remembering Wallace Stegner* (Palo Alto, CA: Stanford University Press, 1996).

"In Memory: Wallace Stegner, 1909–1993" was first published as "Author's legacy extends beyond words of the land to its preservation" in the *San Jose Mercury News*, April 18, 1993.

"Speech After Long Silence" was first published in *The Wilderness Vision: On the Poetry of John Haines*, ed. Kevin Bezner and Kevin Walzer (Ashland, OR: Story Line Press, 1996).

A shortened version of the essay "My Friend Hayden" was published in *American Poet,* fall 2007. The present version ends with several paragraphs from "Hello, Hayden," from *The Sewanee Review*, fall 2009.

"A Master Language" was first published in *The Sewanee Review*, summer 1997.

"Sweetness Preserved" was first published in *"Bright Unequivocal Eye": Poems, Papers, and Remembrances from the first Jane Kenyon Conference*, ed. Bert G. Hornback and Peter Lang (New York: Peter Lang Publishing Group, 2000).

"Some Interim Thoughts about Gary Snyder's *Mountains and Rivers Without End*" was first published in *The Sewanee Review*, winter 1998.

"In Memory: James Baker Hall" was first published in *The Sewanee Review*, winter 2010.

"Against the Nihil of the Age" was first published in *The Sewanee Review*, October–December 2001.

"The Uses of Adversity" was first published in *The Sewanee Review*, April–June 2007.

"God, Science, and Imagination" was first published in *The Sewanee Review*, winter 2010.

# Works Cited

~

*The Bluegrass Region of Kentucky and Other Kentucky Articles* by James Lane Allen (MacMillan); *The Boat of Quiet Hours* by Jane Kenyon (Graywolf Press); *The Collected Poems* by Kathleen Raine (Counterpoint); *The Collected Poems of William Carlos Williams, Volume I, 1909–1939*, ed. A. Walton Litz and Christopher MacGowan (New Directions); *The Collected Poems of William Carlos Williams, Volume II, 1939–1962*, ed. Christopher MacGowan (New Directions); *Collected Pruse* by Patrick Kavanagh (MacGibbon & Kee); *Collected Shorter Poems* by Hayden Carruth (Copper Canyon Press); *Fables and Distances: New and Selected Essays* by John Haines (Graywolf Press); *I'll Take My Stand: The South and the Agrarian Tradition* by Twelve Southerners (Louisiana State University Press); *In My Father's House* by Ernest J. Gaines (Knopf); *In the American Grain* by William Carlos Williams (New Directions); *Mountains and Rivers Without End* by Gary Snyder (Counterpoint); *Old and New Poems* by Donald Hall (Houghton Mifflin); *The Owl in the Mask of the Dreamer: Collected Poems* by John Haines (Graywolf Press); *Second Space* by Czeslaw Milosz (Ecco); *Selected Essays* by Hayden Carruth (Copper Canyon Press); *Selected Writings of Edmund Burke*, ed. Walter J. Bate (Modern Library); *The Stars, the Snow, the Fire: Twenty-five Years in the Alaska Wilderness* by John Haines (Washington Square Press); *Where the Bluebird Sings to the Lemonade Springs: Living and Writing in the West* by Wallace Stegner (Modern Library); *Whitman: Poetry and Prose* by Walt Whitman (Library of America); *William Carlos Williams and James Laughlin: Selected Letters*, ed. Hugh Witemeyer (W. W. Norton); "Without God" by Steven Weinberg (*The New York Review of Books*).